To Lyle - who gave me my self

PREFACE

This book completes an idle promise made to students and myself as retirement from the classroom loomed ahead, "someday I'm going to write a book about these poor girls." One of them in particular, Elisabeth Christine of Brunswick-Bevern who married Frederick the Great of Prussia, eventually became my subject in these pages. The human dramas of the royal families of Europe were a microcosm of society and culture that never failed to engage and fascinate students in history of early modern western civilization classes. Dates and events came into focus like bones of a skeleton that held the flesh of human beings living years and centuries before us, yet sharing the same human nature and motivations of us all. History as an academic subject became an adventure in the past with insights that apply in the present. "Only the names have changed" became our mantra.

I have many to thank for what follows. Students, colleagues and mentors have inspired and enhanced this effort. In particular, but not exclusively, my great encourager Dr. James Covert whose own teaching "taught me how;" Dr.-Ing. Horst Hardenberg who proposed Elisabeth Christine as a notable subject; Dr. Hans Christian Mempel who fleshed her out in Wolfenbüttel; Br. Donald Stabrowski, C.S.C., Ph.D who opened doors to research opportunity; Dr. Alfred Hagemann who conducted me through Elisabeth's beloved Schönhausen and Frederick's favored Potsdam; Dr. Silke Wagener-Fimpel of the Niedersächsisches Landesarchiv Wolfenbüttel who gave me open access to Elisabeth's letters from childhood through her first decade as Queen; my co-editor Dr. Nancy Hinman whose constancy has helped me maintain the faith, and most of all my husband Lyle, a historian himself and ever wisely supportive, who made forty years of travel in Europe possible. I am very grateful to them all and to the many not named here.

INTRODUCTION

Elisabeth Christine of Brunswick-Bevern was one of my "poor girls:" a shy princess born into the showy world of eighteenth century Europe and thrust into marriage with an egocentric crown prince in grim revolt against a match made for all the wrong reasons. No less successful than many present day revolving-door marriages, it survived intact for more than 50 years only by her honest devotion in spite of his determined neglect. Mismatches were then and still are a common tragedy.

In those days, and long before and after, royal daughters suckled docility and obedience along with their wet nurses' milk; a secure childhood, all too brief, played out in a princely incubation. From birth their stock in the dynasty's portfolio began trading on royal family exchanges from London to St. Petersburg, Copenhagen to Vienna. In their way, these girls were nearly as useful as the more preferred sons since they would provide a handshake to sealing the bargain of foreign alliances and treaties.

Long before Marie Antoinette was sacrificed to France for such a purpose, generations of earlier child brides left the family bosom for uncertain futures. In medieval times a bride could be sent home in disgrace if she failed to suit; it happened to Charlemagne's second wife. One of his predecessors, even more disappointed, retained the ears of the bride he returned.

During the Renaissance an adolescent Catherine of Aragon traveled from Granada in southern Spain across the Channel to England to marry an adolescent Tudor, merging the two "comers" of late fifteenth century European states. Not wishing to let his son leap before he himself had a look, ever cautious Henry VII met Catherine's entourage on its way to London, demanding to see the bride. In his mind was the nagging question: what might wily old Ferdinand of Aragon have pawned off on him, along with a down payment dowry?

Only their virginal state and physical capacity concerned the families receiving these girls. The homes they left behind were not much warmer. Their destiny from birth was to leave the nest. Often their personal servants and attendants did not go along into their new lives. Suspicion could and did focus on ties to the old home. Their new husbands were similarly conditioned. If older and possibly wiser they might already have lost a wife and only wed again to get a necessary heir. "Love [was] not a reason for marriage."[1]

Most royal daughters were hostages to fortune, without hope of finding a kindred soul for a mate, often without even finding themselves. The index of marriages in Europe's ruling houses offer piteously few love matches. Romantic love and caring relationships happened more often on the other side of the blanket.

Conventional reasoning mandated that royal courts, even up to the end of the first world war, organized themselves around a leader who personified not necessarily fitness to rule, but legitimate succession to that rule. His queen must occupy a subordinate position, should bring military and political support, cold cash and most importantly an heir. Daughters, always a disappointment, must not crowd out sons. That this worked almost seamlessly is a testament to the family and clan tradition of early modern Europe.

A queen or crown princess was necessary for the continuity and viability of a royal line, but she must recede into the pomp and circumstance of her position like the smallest stitches of a large tapestry. The more of an also-ran she was able to become, the more she could swallow her own self, the more successful and valuable she would be.

Elisabeth Christine lived some two centuries before the end of old Europe, when such ideas were the standard. The world they served was in its last brilliance, like a dying star already consumed while it still appears in the night sky. From the ashes the voices of a new age and among them, feminine voices blazed an agonizingly long trail out of the decaying past toward a better future.

In the press of those myopic years before the "Great War," Great Britain was pondering the heretofore unthinkable measure of votes for women. Among the arguments, both pro and con, The Times of London quoted a letter from a prominent doctor in opposition to both mental and physical evidence supporting the argument, and two days later an answering letter appeared:

After reading Sir Almroth Wright's able and weightly ex-

---

[1] Friedrich Ludwig Müller, "Elisabeth Christine - Kőnigin von Preussen," Monumente 7/8 (1999): 60.

position of women as he knows them the question seems no longer to be 'Should women have votes?' but 'Ought women not to be abolished altogether?' I have been so much impressed . . . that I have come to the conclusion that women should be put a stop to.

We learn from him that in their youth they are unbalanced, that from time to time they suffer from unreasonableness and hypersensitiveness . . . and . . . . Later on in life they are subject to grave and long-continued mental disorders, and, if not quite insane, many of them have had to be shut up. Now this being so, how much happier and better would the world not be if only it could be purged of women? . . . Is the case really hopeless? Cannot science give us some assurance, or at least some grounds of hope, that we are on the eve of the greatest discovery of all - i.e., how to maintain a race of males by purely scientific means?

And may we not look to Sir Almroth Wright to crown his many achievements by delivering mankind from the parasitic, demented, and immoral species which has infested the world for so long?

Yours obediently,

C.S.C.

['One of the Doomed']

Two days later Prime Minister Asquith wrote to his First Lord of the Admiralty, Winston Churchill:

Much the best thing that I have read for a long time on the Woman Question is a short but very pointed letter in *The Times* today signed C.S.C. Have you any clue to the identity of the writer?[2]

Less than a month earlier Clementine S. Churchill had suffered a miscarriage of what might have been her third child.

Even more to the point of this study is the comment of Eleanor

---

[2] Mary Soames, Clementine Churchill, (Don Mills, Ontario: General Publishing Co. Limited, 1979), 79.

Roosevelt: "A man in high public office is neither husband nor father nor friend in the commonly accepted sense of the words."[3] Elisabeth was joined to such a man. Destined for a crown, he had to be supplied with a mate for the sake of continuity, stability and prosperity. Because of that, her lineage, the dowry she would fetch, her very body and self became a public property. Love had no important role, would be denied from the beginning in fact; respect alone was the pinnacle of her hope.

---

[3] Jon Meacham., <u>Franklin and Winston An Intimate Portrait of an Epic Friendship</u> (New York: Random House, 2003), xvii.

ELISABETH CHRISTINE & FREDERICK FAMILY TREE

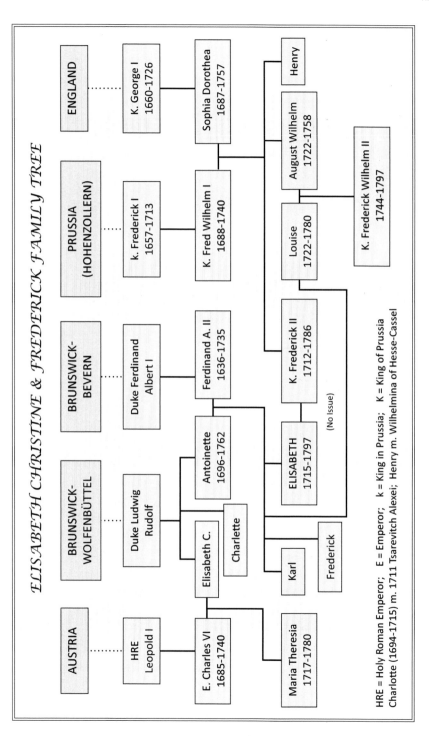

HRE = Holy Roman Emperor;   E = Emperor;   k = King in Prussia;   K = King of Prussia
Charlotte (1694-1715) m. 1711 Tsarevitch Alexei;   Henry m. Wilhelmina of Hesse-Cassel

KEY ROYALS

ALEXEI PETROVICH (1690-1718) Tsarevich of Russia, son of Peter II the Great of Russia.

ANTOINETTE AMALIA (1696-1762) of Brunswick-Wolfenbüttel, daughter of Ludwig Rudolf of Brunswick-Lüneberg, mother of Elisabeth Christine.

ANTON ULRICH (1714-1774) brother of Elisabeth Christine, husband of Anna Leopoldovna (1718-1746), father of Tsar Ivan VI (1740-1764).

AUGUST WILLIAM (1722-1758) Prince of Prussia, brother of Frederick the Great and husband of Luise Amalia of Brunswick-Wolfenbüttel.

CATHERINE II (1729-1796) Tsarina of Russia, born Princess Sophia of Anhalt-Zerbst, married to Tsarevich Peter III.

CHARLES VI (1685-1740) Holy Roman Emperor and father of Maria Theresia.

CHARLOTTE CHRISTINE (1694-1715) of Brunswick-Lüneberg, married to Tsarevich Alexei Petrovich of Russia.

ELISABETH CHRISTINE (1715-1797), Princess of Brunswick-Wolfenbüttel, Queen of Prussia and wife of Frederick II.

ELISABETH CHRISTINE (1691-1750) of Brunswick-Wolfenbüttel, sister of Antoinette Amalia, Holy Roman Empress by her marriage to Holy Roman Emperor Charles VI, Queen of Bohemia and Hungary and mother of Maria Theresia, Empress of Austria and Queen of Hungary.

ELISABETH CHRISTINE ULRIKE (1746-1840) Princess of Brunswick-Wolfenbüttel, Queen of Prussia, divorced 1769 from Frederick William II.

FERDINAND ALBERT II (1680-1735) of Brunswick-Bevern, second son of Ferdinand Albert I of Brunswick-Lüneberg and father of Elisabeth Christine.

FERDINAND (1721-1792) of Brunswick-Bevern and younger brother of Elisabeth Christine, General Field Marshall in Prussian Army.

FREDERICK II (1712-1786), "Fritz" Crown Prince and later King of Prussia, husband of Elisabeth Christine of Brunswick Bevern.

FREDERICK WILLIAM "THE GREAT ELECTOR" (1620-1688) Margrave of Brandenburg, Duke of Cleves, Count of Mark, and Duke of Prussia. Founder of Brandenburg-Prussia following the Thirty Years War.

FREDERICK WILLIAM I (1706-1740) King *in/*of Prussia and father of Frederick II the Great.

FREDERICK WILLIAM II (1744-1797) Crown Prince and later King of Prussia, son of August William Prince of Prussia and Luise Amalia of Brunswick-Wolfenbüttel.

HENRY, PRINCE OF PRUSSIA (1726-1802) younger brother of Frederick the Great, given Schloss Rheinsberg after Frederick became king of Prussia.

KARL I (1713-1780), Duke of Brunswick-Wolfenbüttel, elder brother of Elisabeth Christine, father of Elisabeth Christine Ulrike.

LUDWIG RUDOLF (1671-1735) Duke of Brunswick-Wolfenbüttel, father of Antoinette Amalia and grandfather of Elisabeth Christine.

LUISE AMALIA (1722-1780) Princess of Brunswick-Bevern, Princess of Prussia, wife of August William Crown Prince of Prussia, younger sister of Elisabeth Christine.

MARIA THERESIA (1717-1780), Archduchess of Austria after the death of Charles VI and Queen of Hungary and Bohemia and Holy Roman Empress through husband, Francis I.

PHILIPPINE CHARLOTTE (1716-1801) Princess of Prussia, sister of Frederick II and wife of Karl I of Brunswick-Wolfenbüttel.

SOPHIA DOROTHEA (1687-1757) of Hannover, daughter of George I of England and mother of Frederick II the Great.

WILHELMINE (1709-1758) Princess of Prussia, elder sister of Frederick the Great and wife of Frederick, Margrave of Brandenburg-Bayreuth.

KEY COLLEAGUES

SOPHIE CHARLOTTE de CAMAS (1686-1766) Chief Court Mistress to Elisabeth Christine 1742-1766.

MICHAEL GABRIEL FREDERSDORF (1708-1758) Valet and companion of Fritz.

HANS HERMANN von KATTE (1702-1730) Lt. Prussian Army, close friend and classmate of Fritz, accomplice in escape plan 1730, executed at Küstrin.

DIETRICH von KEYSERLINGK (1698-1778) Fritz nicknamed him Césarion and counted him his best friend.

GEORG WENCESLAS von KNOBELSDORFF (1699-1753) Fritz's friend and Architect from 1740 to 1746.

ERNST AHASVERUS von LEHNDORFF (1727-1811) Chamberlain of Elisabeth Christine from 1767 to 1797.

JOHANN GEORG RITTER von ZIMMERMANN, M.D. (1728-1795) Physician of George III of England and Hanover. Attended Fritz during his last illness.

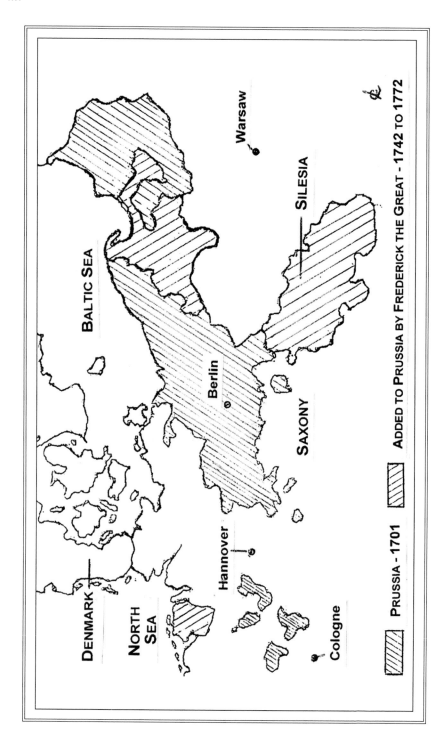

DENMARK

NORTH SEA

BALTIC SEA

Hannover

Berlin

Warsaw

SAXONY

SILESIA

Cologne

PRUSSIA - 1701

ADDED TO PRUSSIA BY FREDERICK THE GREAT - 1742 TO 1772

TABLE OF CONTENTS

CHAPTER ONE

FRIDAY'S CHILD IS LOVING AND GIVING

Ready made for this nursery rhyme's promise, Elisabeth Christine arrived on a Friday, November 8 in 1715, as her father, Ferdinand Albrecht of Brunswick-Bevern* inscribed in the family Bible: "between "six and seven minutes to eight in the morning"[1] in Wolfenbüttel, a graceful little town of half-timbered houses in Lower Saxony. Signs were all promising: parents with a loving marriage[2] and two older brothers who would be her lifelong friends.

Before his marriage Ferdinand had been a soldier, serving as aide-de-camp to the prestigious Eugene of Savoy in the Austrian army. "The Long Bevern"[3] climbed the ranks to general field marshal and governor of the Habsburg fortress at Pressburg., now Bratislava in Slovakia. Along the way, Ferdinand learned political affairs as well as military management from the inside. But when it came to marriage, thirty-two year old Ferdinand left that behind to marry his cousin's granddaughter, sixteen year old Antoinette Amalia of Brunswick. They knew each other well as part of the extended Brunswick family, and affection had grown into love for them both. Oiling the transition, Austria shrewdly recognized that Ferdinand would beyond question squeeze into the ducal chair in Wolfenbüttel when it became empty.

Theirs was an out-of-the-ordinary union. While close bloodline connections were commonplace and May-September pairings nothing special, love matches did not take place very often. However, Antoinette was the youngest of a doting father's three daughters; he had already pulled off impressive coups with two older girls now sitting in chairs next to thrones in Vienna and St. Petersburg. This time a marriage for love could be swallowed, particularly since the bridegroom was sure to follow Antoinette's father, and his uncle, in the Brunswick succession. It was all a neatly wrapped package.

---

*Brunswick-Wolfenbüttel" is hereafter used in preference to the German Braunschweig-Wolfenbüttel.
[1] Paul Noack, <u>Elisabeth Christine und Friedrich der Grosse Ein Frauenleben in Preussen</u> (Stuttgart: Klett-Cotta, 2001) 14.
[2] Herr Gerhardt Ritscher, personal interview, 22 August 2006 in Wolfenbüttel.
[3] Ferdinand was strikingly tall.

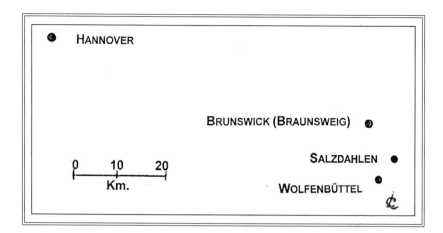

Two sons were born before their second wedding anniversary, Elisabeth came three weeks before their third. She was named for the star of the family, her mother's older sister Elisabeth Christine, wife of the Holy Roman Emperor Charles VI.[4] High connection descended on the baby but not much else. Princely pecking order among the lesser German states such as her own remained well below that of the Habsburg emperors, all born to the top shelf.

Ferdinand's entry in the family's Bible illuminates a rare closeness between a husband and wife of their station. High politics and great estate demanded brilliant marriages, and settled for the cold marriage beds that usually followed. Warmth could come from the other side of the blanket after (sometimes alongside) a dynasty's demands for legitimate heirs. Common sense ordered that such indulgence was only allowed a husband; his wife's chastity insured valid succession.

Over the next eighteen years after 1715 a dozen more children were born, the last coming two years before Ferdinand's death in 1735. Elisabeth fared better than many with childhood and youth spent among a growing family where father and mother took active part in their children's lives. In spite of their princely titles it was a modest life, funded by his modest pension of 12,000 thalers[5] from Austrian service. Small change by Vienna or St. Petersburg standards, it was enough for a com-

---

[4] The middle daughter had married the only legitimate son of Peter the Great.

[5] An approximate appraisal of the North German thaler in the eighteenth century compares the salary of 6,000 thalers per year of the Prussian ambassador to England with the cost of a beet factory built by the Prussian crown for 50,000 thalers.

fortable life in Wolfenbüttel, described as a curious mix of small-town charm and big politics.[6] Tsar Peter II (the Great) called it a paradise on earth during his visit in 1713.

A century before, the town had shrewdly sidestepped Austrian expansion by declaring its neutrality in the Thirty Years War (1618-1648) which was igniting large parts of northern Europe. This early holocaust to destroy Protestantism and turn back history's clock to repossess former personal and Roman Catholic church properties ultimately backfired. Christians of both persuasions as well as kings and knaves stepped forward not necessarily for piety's cause, but for real estate and the spoils of war. When it finally ended in 1648 another generation had been born and matured, inured by the horrors and death that laid waste to much of central Europe. Wolfenbüttel's submission thirty years earlier prevented the worst of atrocities taking place there.

Ferdinand's grandfather, Duke August the Younger (1579-1666), took on Wolfenbüttel's reconstruction after the war ended and by his death in 1666 most of the damage had been put to right. August the "younger," actually youngest, son was born with little chance to become Duke, but possessed a brilliant mind which led to his study at the universities of Tübingen, Rostock and Strassburg as well as lengthy travels in France, England and Italy. To the great good fortune of future generations of scholars, he began collecting books in a systematic way through agents all over Europe, eventually building up a personal collection of well over 130,000 volumes and manuscripts by the end of his life. When the duchy came into his hands he brought this library with him to join the collection of his grandfather and father and all of it became a public one. Its rare and outstanding research collections of medieval and early modern intellectual history continue to be a major destination for serious scholars.

Anton Ulrich, August's heir continued supporting the library but added his own greater passion, the current aristocratic fad of building a pleasure palace nearby in the spirit of Versailles. Its showiness paid for from shallower pockets led to on the cheap construction, far inferior to the Versailles model. Salzdahlum's glory would not last long past the next century. However, Anton possessed two other assets who turned out to be priceless and thrust his family a giant step upward into the

---

6 Noack, 15.

first rank of European monarchy. In 1692 he began negotiations to bring his granddaughters forward where his sons could not go. In due course they married the prestigious Habsburg and Romanov crown princes.

The eldest, Elisabeth Christine (namesake of her future niece), was sent to Vienna in 1708 to marry the Archduke Charles VI, next in line to become Holy Roman Emperor. Three years later the middle girl, Charlotte Christine went to Thorn in Poland to marry Tsar Peter the Great's only son Alexis. The lone advantage in this pig-in-a-poke union was that Charlotte could keep her Protestant religion; any children, however, must be raised in the Russian Orthodox faith.[7] It was a cold hearted affair from the start; Alexis was repelled by a German wife and her German entourage. He began searching, in his turn and by his father's example, beyond the blanket for more appetizing fare. It was not Alexis' first nor only rebellion and finally Wolfenbüttel's Russian connection was ruptured in the flashpoint of Peter's fury.

The Tsar himself supervised Alexis's torture and death in his new high security prison, the Fortress of St. Peter and St. Paul in St. Petersburg. By that time a three year old son and future heir had come along to validate Alexis and Charlotte's union. Something might have been salvaged for Wolfenbüttel had Charlotte not died shortly after her son was born. Instead she went to a grave under the bell tower of the Cathedral within the Fortress where her husband had died in agony; her family's failed luck-of-the-draw seemed to be buried along with her.

The Wolfenbüttel's had better luck in Vienna. Though only granddaughters resulted from Elisabeth Christine's marriage to Charles, one of them, Maria Theresia with her more than stalwart character underneath a beautiful blond exterior, was enough. Commanding blue eyes betrayed the will of iron and bone-deep sense of purpose within. Her far less gifted father bewailed his lack of a son until his dying day in 1740, but he could not have provided better for the dicey job of ruling a multi-ethnic, open-to-hostile-takeover state such as Austria was in the eighteenth century.

Marriage to Antoinette had not yet fixed Ferdinand's place in the political picture. As the first son of a third son from a second marriage of a Duke of Brunswick-Wolfenbüttel in the previous generation, Ferdi-

---

[7] Lindsay Hughes, <u>The Romanovs Ruling Russia 1613-1917</u> (London: Hambledon Continuum, 2008) 72.

nand stood in a line of tangled succession until 1735 when the issue was buried along with his father-in-law, Ludwig Rudolf, and he was awarded the title. Without the glitter and gold of Vienna or St. Petersburg and its cynical compromising opportunism, their family living within financial constraint and small society were personal blessings for Ferdinand and Antoinette in their first home, an apartment in the Kleines Schloss in Wolfenbüttel, also called the Princes Court. It perfectly suited Antoinette's home-loving nature and her growing brood. Living across the moat from the ducal palace and separated from the protocol of court life, their little Elisabeth Christine had the better of two worlds. Most royal as well as noble babies went straight from birth into their own households with wet nurse and governess, in rooms set well apart from their parents. The loftier their station and larger the palace meant the farther away they were. But Ferdinand and Antoinette lived with closer quarters and stricter means; eventually they took the upbringing and education of their children into their own hands, the father with the sons and the mother with the daughters. At early ages the children were exposed to Bible stories and the conversations with learned theologians who visited their grandparents' court in the Schloss. When she was six years old Elisabeth was given a red leather bound Bible belonging to her mother for her own. The earnest, religious spirit which pervaded the Kleines Schloss during her childhood and beyond never left her.[8]

Apart from spiritual matters, and in spite of Wolfenbüttel's renowned library and the scholars drawn to it, Ferdinand and Antoinette felt that very high standards and teachers were much less important for daughters than for sons. Elisabeth's French teacher, for example, was inadequate and her own competence in the language continued to be inadequate when she married. Since all the courts of Europe communicated in that elegant, circuitous language it would put her on the wrong foot were she to marry upward as her aunts had done. More an impediment, she never expressed herself well in writing, even in her native German. Offsetting this laxity though, her parents created a genuine fondness and family feeling that other children of privilege lacked, giving her the self-esteem to accept life as it would come.

---

[8] Paula Joepchen, <u>Die Gemahlin Friedrichs des Grossen Elisabeth Christine als Schriftstellerin</u> (Köln: Druckeri M. Mundelsee, 1939). 7.

She could be herself, a gift that not all parents can bestow. Home was a warm nest that she cherished in memory, but its benefits never excused her intellectual inadequacy in the eyes of the gifted but driven Frederick of Prussia. Writers of royal marriage contracts never took into account imbalanced pairings such as Frederick and Elisabeth's. Education was an irrelevant issue when it came to women; lower orders could not spare a daughter's time away from household chores, and higher castes believed development of a female's mind not only a waste of time, but often dangerous. Even those directly in line to reign were neglected in this way. Elisabeth Christine's cousin Maria Theresia in Vienna ultimately succeeded her father, ill-educated and unbriefed, to take up the sagging state he left her. Determination and common sense practicality eventually saw her through, but at the start an empty treasury and shopworn army nearly ended her reign, and Austria's prospects, before it began.[9]

Elisabeth possessed artistic talent, obviously encouraged, looking at her self-portrait of 1738 in comparison with one of the same year by the Prussian court painter, Antoine Pesne. Her own work aided by Pesne's advice shows a simplicity of character that escaped the professional's work.[10] Her singing voice, too, was trained by the court musician, Johann Gottlieb Graun, but no instrumental ability was developed. Just as well, her future husband became a serious musician and competition from his wife in that sphere would have been a nagging thorn in Fritz's ego. At least Graun was esteemed highly enough to be hired away from Wolfenbüttel by the court at Berlin.[11]

Ultimately fifteen children were born to Antoinette and Ferdinand, the last coming six months after Elisabeth's marriage. A small court such as Wolfenbüttel's must cut the cloth to fit the means and fifteen children stretched that fabric to its maximum. Offsetting that, twenty-one years of childbearing had not faded Antoinette and Ferdinand's devotion to each other. Ferdinand was a true "house and children's father."[12] New

---

[9] A generation later she failed one of her own children in the same way, sending Marie Antoinette into the maelstrom of Versailles with only a pretty face and figure to shield the sparse education of a fifteenth child.

[10] Günter Rieger, <u>Elisabeth Christine Gattin Friedrichs II von Preussen</u> (Nördlingen: Druckerei Steinmeier, 1999) 29, 31.

[11] Joepchen, 8.

[12] Noack, 17.

babies were always announced by Ferdinand himself, sounding for all the world like Victorian fathers a century later. "Children, your mother is very ill," he would declare and then direct them to pray with him.[13] Within a few hours he would return with the news of a baby sister or brother's arrival.

The cocoon would not be isolated, though. Ferdinand had lived too close to Eugene of Savoy and the court in Vienna to forget his obligation to dynastic interest. Charles XII of Sweden and Tsarevitch Alexis of Russia became godfathers of his eldest son, Karl. Looking out for the prospects of his brood mandated compromise on several levels, and Ferdinand was a man of his world. When his daughters married he would accept new religions for them, even different lifestyles if need be. In the meantime Ferdinand would try to live within his income in order to make his home secure. His single indulgence was a small regiment he drilled regularly, reminding him of his youth.

It was the tenor of the times to think of children as future fortune for the family as well as themselves, not for their own sake alone. Daughters especially were Hochzeitsware, "goods for weddings," i.e. political capital. Elisabeth, her brothers Karl and Anton and younger sisters Luise Amalia and Juliane all married upward into the Prussian, Russian and Danish royal families. Maximizing offsprings' opportunities was any parent's duty, but in Wolfenbüttel's case, the warmth of a father and mother who took pride in their children enveloped the marriage plans they made.

All this could hardly have been in sharper contrast to the arrogant spite of the neighboring royal family in Berlin. No matter, the future was nearly at hand. It was already too late to consider personal feelings and individual abilities in light of the political designs of Prussia and Austria. Elisabeth's suitable family House, her known quantity father, and even better her mother, a sister of the Emperor's wife in Vienna, all placed her on Berlin's short list. It suited Vienna's policy as well and they kept wedding bells jangling in Ferdinand's head. Elisabeth, untried and obedient, was to be handed off to a new life whose parameters she hardly knew existed. Its promise of high estate would make her Queen of Prussia all too soon and without a sustaining partner beside her.

---

[13] Noack, 19.

CHAPTER TWO

EIN PLUS MACHEN*

Connections were crucial to the newly assigned "kingdom" of Prussia in 1701. The House of Hohenzollern, a rising power in the Germanies[1] had been grappling its way upward for more than 80 years. Once arrived at their goal, stability and staying power demanded a bride for the son of its king, Crown Prince Frederick with an heir and as many "spares" as possible. Royal status could not afford to consider less. Brides could be pretty and pleasant or homely and spiteful; such details were irrelevant. Essential was a well-connected and prolific succession that would stake their claim to bona fide sovereignty.

Elisabeth Christine of Brunswick-Wolfenbüttel met the imperative for Frederick William I (1688-1740), King of Prussia. He knew her father well and thought he would gain the best material available in a daughter-in-law. Sadly, his simplistic goals fell far short of the mark and the marriage itself doomed father, son and bride to years of grinding frustration. Concern with bloodline alone was endemic to all ruling families, the past thereby fated the future. The high and mighty of Europe demanded that sons and daughters accept whatever expedient marriage options were available. Cold dynastic planning was blind to personal fancy, genetic flaws or even religion, which all was " . . . prostituted to unite titles and estates."[2] Annulment for sufficient reasons of state had always been on tap, just in case, and continued to be.

Originally, during the middle ages as on-the-make Counts of Zollern in southwestern Germany, they had grabbed the main chance when offered control of the territory of Brandenburg, south of the Baltic Sea, by the Holy Roman Emperor Sigismund in 1417. Proven military skill and staying power were being rewarded with land and responsibilities in time-worn feudal practice. No overlord ever gave away a fief great

---

* MAKE A PROFIT: the instinctive mantra of the Hohenzollern efficiency model.

[1] Germany, as a unified nation, did not exist until 1871, following the Franco-Prussian War. Before then it was know as "the Germanies" denoting the particularist structure of central Europe's German areas.

[2] Abigail Adams' sharp observation in 1784 in David McCullough, <u>John Adams</u>, (New York: Simon & Schuster, 2001), 303.

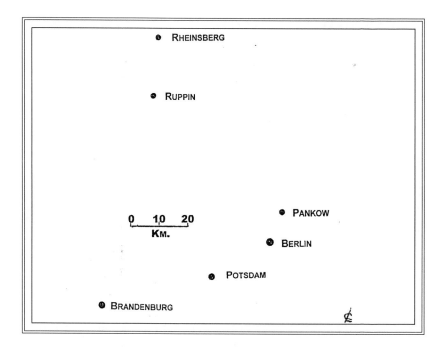

or small without iron expectations. Thus the Zollerns of Swabia, with a new place to stand, transformed themselves into the Hohenzollern, i.e. "high" Zollern Electors or Princes of Brandenburg.

Less than a century later another Hohenzollern added to the family's holdings when he became the last Grand Master of the Teutonic Knights in 1511, finally reigning Duke of East Prussia in 1525 when the Order was dissolved. Brandenburg was joined with East Prussia, an underwhelming territory of sand and swampy bog. It was only improved over time by the labor of peasants recruited from the west and bankrolled by the ruling family's investment of enough land and farming equipment to exploit its potential. Virtually land-locked, the new state eventually bordered on the eastern Baltic Sea, never a major trade outlet, while to the south Habsburg Austria kept it in bounds, as Poland did in the east.

The Zollern's climb was only beginning. From now on they needed to work harder and smarter, be leaner and meaner against their rivals among the petty German states, and all of the family must be put to use, either in force of arms or fecundity. Personal sacrifice was expected and coerced if need be. Only such a resolute sense of mission over the next two centuries brought them to the biting edge of greatness. "Ein plus machen" became reality through the prolific energy of Frederick William, the "Great Elector" who had brought his lands out of the devastation left behind by the Thirty Years War and labored doggedly to hand it on to his son Frederick, re-built and enlarged in size. It had not been easy; Prussia faced threats by Sweden, Poland and the Dutch Republic, all ready to grab away as much as they could. A tough fighting force, disciplined and well run, was vital. During his reign beginning in 1640 his army grew from 3,000 to 38,000 by 1688 when he died. Improved tactics and armaments along with good leadership led to a low desertion rate and respected status for the military machine of Hohenzollern.

First among the resulting profits was a new appellation, "King *in* Prussia" for his heir Frederick William I, bartered in 1701 in exchange for the use of Prussia's army by The Holy Roman Emperor Leopold I. The title swap came about because Louis XIV of France had tried a power play to put a spoke in the wheels of Austria, Prussia and England and bend their wills to French design. Louis' brother-in-law, the dimly lit Carlos II, King of Spain, was childless and in pitiful health.

Carlos's only heirs were his sisters, Leopold's wife and Louis' wife. The elder woman was the Holy Roman Empress and the younger, Queen of France. By right of primogeniture Leopold's wife would inherit the Spanish Crown, but cocksure ambition goaded Louis XIV to force the claim of his own unappetizing wife, until now consoling herself with chocolates and garlic, it was said, while Louis sampled the charms of women of the court. But Maria Teresa could be of some value after all by bringing all of Spain into Louis' hands. There are no longer any Pyrenees, bragged Louis.

England, the Netherlands, Austria and Spain would not stand by as France took over a third of western Europe; thirteen years of war ensued and finally was settled by a compromise three years after Louis died. His grandson would wear the Spanish crown but lost all rights in France; the Pyrenees remained the border between the two countries. Various land and cash perks were parceled out to the rest of the powers to sweeten bargains made and level the European playing field. Frederick William's own troops-for-title deal paid off by finally getting the crown *of* Prussia, his principal aim in the first place.

Using the same given name for eldest sons over succeeding generations has been a tiresome habit, but should not blur the contrasting personalities, often diametrically opposed. The Great Elector's son, Frederick I (1657-1713), patterned his court after the glitzy style of Versailles, to the extent of engaging a mistress with whom he walked every afternoon. After nightfall the charade would end since he slept only with his wife. The newly royal Frederick crowned himself and afterwards placed a crown on his wife's head: not gallantry, but visually and politically putting her on the second rung of his ladder.

Overdone ceremonial was life's blood to this Hohenzollern and his extravagant coronation that cost some six million thalers, twice Prussia's annual revenue, nearly emptied the state treasury. At the same time, his capital of Berlin got newly paved streets and fine buildings, to bring all but the treasury up to par. Such excess was not lost on his thirteen year old son, an ingrained pinchpenny. At the king's death in 1713, his son paid for an extravagant funeral, but when it was over all costly rituals were retired and locked away in memory. Frederick William I's reign would begin with frugality, and from then on the elegance of Bourbon France found no welcome in Hohenzollern Berlin. Stiff shirtsleeves to stiff shirtsleeves had returned, Ein Plus Machen was back.

Seven years earlier Frederick William had married Sophia Dorothea, daughter of George I of England. By 1713 they had two small children: four year old Frederike Wilhelmine and year old, yet another, Frederick. Before that they had lost two baby boys and after little Fritz's birth further sons were slow to arrive; five living daughters came before their last three sons were born.

Fritz was an unpromising baby, a great worry to his parents whose hopes and plans were focused on his puny self. He was the last satisfaction of a prodigal grandfather's life; typically, the old man honored it by encasing the baby's umbilical cord in a silver gilt container inscribed with name, date and time of the birth and placed in the Berlin museum.[3] Fritz and his big sister Wilhelmina came to be the acknowledged senior partners in an eventual large number of siblings. Above all the rest they coveted each other's company and sought each other's loyalty and opinions during childhood and beyond.

Their father and mother were both extraordinarily selfish and thick

---

[3] Time and the tides of war seem to have swallowed up this relic.

skinned. He grew up ill-mannered and self-indulgent, showing little promise of the taskmaster of a no-frills Prussia he became. However, after years of his father's fusty ceremonial, the king set a course toward a new system of rule with himself the chief of finance, church administration, education and legal affairs. Like a religious convert he not only threw his energy into these offices but vowed to bring along his heir so that the line of efficiency from the top down would not be broken. Woe to a son that did not live up to that high calling; woe to the son who eventually did.

Since the mother of his children was the sister of his childhood rival, George II of England, she was definitely not the choice of his romantic desires. But he swallowed his disappointment and accepted the hard fact that queens existed for only one purpose: to produce an heir and as many more as heaven might send. In their case the number was fourteen, with four lost in early infancy. The impressive total demonstrates the absence of a royal mistress, perhaps another element of practical efficiency: "Use it up, make it do, or do without," the frugality model of the 1930's, aptly describes Frederick William's no-nonsense philosophy and his attitude toward his family as well as his job. Whatever the case, the marriage existed at best as an armed truce and at worst as a series of violent scenes throughout their thirty-four years together.

Childhood under the rule of such a pair could be brutal, and if Wilhelmina's letters are an indication, the two elder children suffered fear and humiliation, even physical violence, at the hands of a tinder-box father. Each parent had dynastic and political plans to use their children like state property. From that perspective, the cycle of advantageous marriage, production of children followed by early betrothals, consumed every royal parent from bridal bed to death bed. In Frederick William and his wife's case their ambitions polarized and life in the palace became a no-man's land between them.

Sophia Dorothea set her heart on a marriage between her daughter and her brother's son, the Prince of Wales, followed by Fritz's wedding to her brother's daughter Anne. Frederick William had no wish for marriage with England catching any of his children, much less his valuable eldest son. Years before he had taken a strong hostility to his wife's brother when they were children, bloodying his nose in a boyish scuffle and some reported nearly biting off his ear. Later on, roles reversed when George bested Frederick by acquiring Frederick's first love, Caroline of Ansbach, as a bride. It was only hard-nosed reality; Caroline's family had looked to their own prospects, giving her to a promising England instead of a backwater Prussia. Salting the wound, George's sister Sophia Dorothea was sent to Berlin as Frederick William's bride.

As their family grew, planning for their futures occupied both parents. Sophia Dorothea's plans came to the notice of the Austrian ambassador to Prussia, Count Friedrich von Seckendorff, who met this strategic risk by pressing on Frederick William the urgency of aligning with Austria instead of England in the marriage of his eldest son. For Frederick William, loyalty to his Emperor in Vienna was a keystone of his integrity as a German prince. Going against several hundred years of Hohenzollern loyalty to the Empire was not to be thought of; Sophia Dorothea lost her battle before she could land a blow. She managed, however, to hang onto her spite.

Austria possessed another ace in the hole, a "mole" bought and paid on a regular basis, within the close circle of Frederick William's council. Baron General Frederick William Grumbkow, chief minister and advisor to the King, had become close to Count Seckendorff, fed by their common fear of England and the secret payments Grumbkow received from Vienna. In time the two men moved into young Fritz's orbit and Grumbkow particularly became a confidant to the prince who would be his King one day.

Frederick William and Sophia Dorothea's frequent quarreling made for a stormy family life, physically violent at times with the two eldest bearing the brunt of their father's rage and frustration. Fritz was subjected to toughening up with rigid military discipline in order to offset what seemed to be his frail constitution. Wilhelmine did not escape her share, her father often yanking her around by the hair. The king honestly believed that his son could only rule Prussia in the future if any pampering his mother provided was offset by a father's endless critical appraisals. Long before it might have been needed, this tough love was taken to the maximum.

The king had never spared himself either. As a boy of nine when he was given his own estate at Wusterhausen, fifty miles (80 km.) southeast of Berlin, he had to learn how to manage it. By the age of thirteen he was sitting in his father's Privy Council and at twenty he had become vocal about the state corruption he witnessed.[4] When the rule of Prussia came into his hands, he was determined to re-order the government toward prosperity in his lifetime. To lead by example he paid taxes to the state just as he expected his subjects to do, and monitored court and bureaucratic spending with the zeal of an economic tyrant. Securing these gains for the future meant pouring his raw determination into the rough clay of his eldest son, toughening him by cannon fire at dawn and filling his days with military drill.

Unreasonable expectations very often led to arbitrary, cruel punishment accompanied by withering sarcasm heaped upon the Crown Prince's head. Through bitter experience Fritz learned to accept his lot in silence but that very passivity enraged his father. Following one appalling scene the king manhandled his son to the floor, forcing him to kiss the royal boots and then roared "If my father had treated me like this I would have put an end to my life long ago. But you have no courage."[5] It was a barbarous childhood and it succeeded in coiling a spring of steel resolve within young Fritz. At one point he told his sister Wilhelmine that he would rather beg for food than go on living.

By mid-July of 1730 eighteen year old Fritz believed his longed-for chance to escape had finally come. For some time he had been requesting money to pay for it from an envoy of his uncle, George II. When the King of England finally approved the funds to be handed over Fritz determined to melt away into exile. A golden opportunity opened when his father allowed him to join a royal tour of south Germany and Fritz grasped it. Letting a few of his closest friends in on the plan, particularly twenty-four year old Hans Hermann von Katte, Fritz headed off in the van for what he naively thought would become ultimate freedom in England. Still an adolescent, he never considered that a welcome there might be lukewarm at best. George II would only have seen his nephew as an embarrassment; paying off debts was all the help he intended to give.

In any case none of it happened. The son's will was not equal to the father's iron control. Frederick William found out about the plan and demanded a complete explanation. Fritz was thoroughly terrified; it

[4] Christopher Clark, <u>Iron Kingdom The Rise and Downfall of Prussia 1600-1947</u> (Cambridge: Harvard University Press, 2006), 86.
[5] Ludwig Reiners, <u>Frederick the Great An Informal Biography</u> (New York: G. P. Putnam's Sons, 1960), 32.

was a known fact that a dozen years before the Russian Tsar Peter II had brutally tortured and killed his son and heir for an attempt to escape his destiny. After four hearings, with Fritz again and again covering his true intentions to the last, his father, in cold fury, ordered Fritz removed under escort and elaborate precautions to Küstrin, a military fortress on the east bank of the Oder river, fifty miles (80 km.) east of Berlin. Escape would be impossible. In the event of trouble along the way, he was to be surrendered "nothing other than dead"[6] by sovereign order. Von Katte, so dear to Fritz's heart would ultimately pay that ominous price on 6 November. With a grenadier stationed at Fritz's side to prevent any part of the scene being missed from the window of his cell, Katte was beheaded in the courtyard of Küstrin castle. It was a vindictive act by a man determined to bring his son to heel, but it hardened a heart fully as determined to endure and bide its time.

Rehabilitation into Frederick Williams' good graces and trust would be long and painful. Any "comforts" were forbidden, such as his flute and his books, except for three volumes: the Bible, a hymnal and an approved book, True Christianity, and of course absolutely no taint of Calvinism's pre-destination. His physical self needed shaping up as well; the Bösewicht[7] affected long hair, walked like a ballet dancer, ate sloppily and didn't keep himself clean. Whether Fritz had to unlearn bad habits or give in his stubborn penchant for annoying his father, at all events more than a year was to pass before Fritz's Prussian army uniform was restored to him, let alone a return to his standing before the summer of 1730 at court.

In mid-November he was given the lowest position in Küstrin's provincial administration and told to learn, from the ground up, the scope of the Hohenzollern domain from agriculture and animal husbandry to tax collection and land use. This flighty and rebellious son must come to understand his inheritance from hands-on experience. Fritz had to

---

[6] Giles MacDonogh, Frederick the Great A Life in Deed and Letters. (New York: St. Martin's Press, 1999), 65. As noted in Reinhold Koser, Geschichte des Friedrichs des Grossen. (Darmstadt: Wissenschaftliche Buchgesellschaft, 1963), 1: 44, and Carl Hinrichs, Der Kronprinzenprozess: Friedrich und Katte. (Hamburg: Hanseatische Verlagsanstalt, 1936), 37-8.
[7] the "scoundrel." in Robert B. Asprey, Frederick the Great The Magnificent Enigma (New York: Ticknor & Fields, 1986), 78.

face himself and put dreams of glory unearned out of his mind. It was a tall order but he got his feet under him and began sending his father reports of what he was learning about the land and life of the province. It must have kept some hope alive that Fritz would, after all, be saved.

Frederick William saw his own mission in the growth and prosperity of Brandenburg-Prussia and that necessarily included his heir. A thriving economy and a single-minded will was necessary to move the Hohenzollern state upward into the Austrian-Russian-English orbit. His son could not escape his destiny as the second King of Prussia and Frederick William was determined to make him ready for it.

The other rehabilitation must be marriage to an already chosen bride, with no complaints allowed about her personal qualities or intellectual gifts. This gadfly of an heir would be carrot-and-sticked into his dynastic duty. So began the corporate side of a union: the marriage contract. In the eighteenth century fathers negotiated this business pact in which a girl traded her name and share of her family inheritance for her husband's name; in return her father gave a sum of money and total control of it into the hands of her new family. From it her annual allowance and other needs would be met.

The negotiations over, Elisabeth Christine's fate was sealed in early 1732 as she arrived in Berlin at the invitation of Fritz's younger sister Charlotte, the fiancée of her brother Karl. Elisabeth had not been told about her marriage project and Frederick William arbitrarily decided that his daughter could break the news. Looking back at the litany of thoughtlessness that was going to become her lot as time went on, it is at least good to know that her father would have none of that. He and his wife would tell their daughter what had been decided. The king gave in; his liking for the girl had gotten through the slave driver's tough hide. From then on through the rest of his life, Frederick William was as much of a kind friend to her as he was able to be.

Simple and unaffected, raised in simplicity and stability, how could she realize that the well advanced warfare between King and Crown Prince would infect her relations with both of them and while she might well please the father she never would engage the son?

CHAPTER THREE

BAGGAGE IN THE VAN

Snares and pitfalls clouded over Elisabeth and Fritz as they and their families made their way to Salzdahlum. Their marriage was designed to serve what Frederick William coveted: a seat at the Head Table of European politics. Prussia's assets were impressive: a standing army and stable treasury presided over by a hard-working, iron headed monarch. To the greedy eyes of England and Habsburg Austria it was too valuable to ignore.

Fritz who would inherit those assets, along with their burdens, had survived a tough school from early childhood, and this marriage seemed to be further bondage since his father had hand-picked the bride. Still, he knew it had to be endured. Frederick William had sized up the field of girls available to strike the sharpest bargain. If he had opted for an English match, and followed his wife's desires, his smaller Prussia would become a mere satellite and Russia had nothing better to offer than an unequal match and succession issues impossible to solve.

Fritz looked at his prospects differently. Austria was his long shot favorite but even his outsize ego had to face facts. The "Austrian Empire" was an ethnic ragout ruled over by the German Habsburg dynasty that, by the 18th century, included Hungary's Magyars, Bohemia's Czechs and Slovaks, Galicia's Poles, Slavs in Ruthenia and Slovenes and Serbo-Croats in the Balkans. The emperor, Charles VI, would never give up his historical leverage over Prussia even though he had only a female heir and a paper guarantee[1] from the rest of Europe to secure his borders. Political reality dictated that Prussian troops were worth more than signatures on a document. However, because Frederick William's loyalty had never come into question, there was no need for Charles to waste his daughter on a tag-along Hohenzollern.

Fritz was caught between a rock and a hard place; his pride and sense of destiny were small change against the size and dominance

---

[1] The Pragmatic Sanction of 1713 was an agreement by the major powers of Europe to respect the territorial integrity of Austria and her possessions should Charles VI be succeeded by a female heir. The old Salic Law of the early sixth century that forbid female rule had long been overruled.

of his neighbors. Hohenzollerns maintained their status because they clung tightly to the Habsburgs' coattails. That reality justified the past, but Fritz had the future in his sights. Frederick William's choosing of the Wolfenbüttel daughter galled him but he must grit his teeth clamped around the bit of his father's determination, and soldier on.

The choice best served the interests of all. Prussia gained in-law status in the Habsburg family since Elisabeth was Charles VI's wife's niece. Fritz was already filling his ever empty pockets with an allowance from Charles and should not expect more. Others in his family and entourage were also receiving Austrian money.[2] Frederick William had no stomach for wasting his heir or his dynasty's status. There was no other decision to make: both country and son would best be served by a bride who was a nonentity. Sons she must provide, not competition. Elisabeth, then, was a handshake that maintained the old balance of power.

She had never left Wolfenbüttel and its environs before marriage plans were talked of. Only when she was sixteen did she see a bit of the larger world on a visit with her mother to relatives 130 miles (208 km.) away in Hamburg. It was planned to polish her up a bit, but Elisabeth came down with smallpox there and returned home somewhat blemished and still not polished. At most, Hamburg could not have opened her sheltered eyes as sixteen year old Fritz's had been two years before at Dresden's opulent, grossly self-indulgent court of Augustus the Strong, Elector of Saxony.

At the time, Frederick William was dead set against his son tagging along to Dresden's carnival in the late winter of 1728, prophetically assuming the worst. Once there Fritz leapt into the drunken revels, falling in love with Augustus' beautiful natural daughter. A complaisant Augustus, who shared his own bed with her at times, allowed it to happen.[3] The result of whatever kind of liaison this became is difficult, but surely tempting, to judge. Without doubt something fateful happened since Fritz's return from Dresden in 1728 was marked by an illness serious enough that Georg Stahl, professor of medicine at the University of Halle, was called to Berlin. Several weeks of emetics and enemas

---

[2] Ludwig Reiners, <u>Frederick the Great A Biography</u> (New York: G.P. Putnam's Sons, 1960) 66.
[3] Augustus is thought to have sired more than three hundred fifty bastards.

along with cure-all bloodlettings of the day followed before the patient rallied. Some years later a different doctor reported that his private parts and potency were impaired.[4] Whatever took place, an adolescent Fritz "saw Paree"[5] during that spring and returned to Berlin far more changed than his intended bride's mild case of smallpox would have changed her.

Elisabeth could only bring a third-rate dowry into her marriage: A wedding necklace of 238 pearls provided by her mother's parents, and 25,000 thalers that her grandfather Ludwig Rudolf had drawn from his 150,000 vassals in Wolfenbüttel as a Lady's Tax.[6] Frederick William gave an equal amount since he was so pleased with the girl. Although her father could not provide more money, her Imperial connection to Vienna was a significant asset. Elisabeth herself brought an honest desire to be a caring and generous helpmate and a part of the Prussian royal family.

The stubborn bridegroom, in his own eyes much more than a mere princess from tiny Wolfenbüttel had any right to expect, presented his aloof and distant self. His father, anxious to sweeten the prospect and very aware of Fritz's usual empty pockets, pledged to provide the traditional *Handpfennig*, petty cash, for her pocket money. Always in the red, Fritz's own allowance was spoken for long before he received it.

His last bachelor days were a wry celebration with extravagant food, drink and entertaining at his army post. Frederick William could only hope for wedlock's steadying influence, and to clear the slate he paid all his son's bills before the marriage. Fritz might learn to pinch his pennies in time, but most always he looked toward other pockets than his own. When the Crown finally came to him, *ein plus machen* was ingrained.

After their betrothal in Berlin in March of 1732, the marriage contract was not actually signed by the king of Prussia until the week

---

[4] No royal physician or medical expert would have risked candid remarks about Fritz's prognosis.

[5] The post World War I popular ditty, "How 'Ya Gonna Keep 'Em Down on the Farm, after They've seen Paree?" aptly applies here. [http:// www.usgennet.org/usa/mo/county/.../downonthefarm.htm]

[6] Friedrich Ludwig Müller, "Elisabeth Christine Kőnigin von Preußen II Der schöne Schein" <u>Monumente</u> 7/8 (1999): 59. She was also to receive an annual allowance of 7,200 thalers as Crown Princess, which would become 12,000 annually when she produced an heir.

before the wedding, set for the twelfth of June, 1733. Endless *pas de quatre* movements of the changeable foreign relations between Berlin, Vienna, London and St. Petersburg, clouded over by the haze of French aggrandizement, were responsible for Frederick William's delay. Once those larger issues seemed to be resolved, Fritz complained, after meeting his betrothed and her family, about the corpus delicti being foisted off on him. She was pitiful enough, but her mother was a bigot. Such quibbling mattered little to anyone by this time. His father was determined. Nothing could change that, but at least the blame for his bride's coming isolation, he rationalized, would not be his.

In light of all, it was surely not a match made in heaven but was probably the best that earthly negotiators could arrange. The king found the girl well-trained, decently brought up and God fearing. He did not try to build up her charms; she was neither beautiful nor ugly. However, she was a god-fearing Christian and exactly fit the king's concern on that score. Fritz, a budding atheist, took more comfort in her description as shy, provincial and awkward. She would never pass muster as a mate, but in time she could be useful as a hedge against his father's stubborn management, and even some leverage against his siblings. In the end Elisabeth, "the abominable object of my desire"[7] as the new husband called her, and Frederick were stuck with each other by every argument except that of common humanity.

Her meager household was to number barely twenty persons.[8] The most important post, that of Oberhofmeisterin or Chief Stewardess, was given to Elisabeth von Katsch, widow of a Brunswick pastor. She had been chosen to guide the new Crown Princess as a motherly friend,[9] surely the human influence most sorely needed by an untried young girl. Katsch was also expected to apply the polish about which Frederick and his family continued to nag Grumbkow and Seckendorff.

Besides Frau von Katsch, there were two ladies of nobility, a court steward, a secretary, two pages and a dance teacher. The latter was of the same opinion as the future in-laws, "She dances like a goose."[10]

---

[7] Asprey, 87.
[8] Paul Noack, <u>Elisabeth Christine und Friedrich der Grosse Ein Frauenleben in Preussen</u> (Stuttgart: Klett-Cotta, 2001), 56.
[9] Noack, 55.
[10] Noack, 54.

None were disposed to recognize that the tall girl's gawkiness in mid-adolescence would in time become the regal presence of a queen. Her household staff consisted of three footmen for herself, two chamber maids, a seamstress, a laundress to be aided by another footman, a maid for the stewardess and another footman to serve her noble ladies. This group ought to be more than adequate for any young woman, but its size in the eighteenth century made plain the status of the bride when contrasted with that of her cousin Marie Antoinette, who was sent off to France some years later in a van of fifty-seven coaches drawn by 376 horses, with 200,000 florins and jewels of an equal amount on board.[11] To cover her future, a widow's income of 20,000 gold écus and jewels worth 100,000 écus had been promised.[12] Her trousseau, to be made in France for the wife of its future king, Louis XVI, amounted to $465,000 in twenty-first century terms.[13] Looked at in comparison, the largesse of both Brunswick-Wolfenbüttel and Hohenzollern was pretty small purse.

When Elisabeth and her parents got to Berlin it was sadly obvious to everyone that she had no adequate table talk to display before his critical mother and siblings. Sophia Dorothea, smarting from the rebuff to her English marriage hopes, could only see Elisabeth as stupid and silly, with an annoying nervous giggle. Fritz's sister Phillipine Charlotte claimed after visiting Elisabeth's bedroom that there must be a dozen or so fistulas, suppurating abesses, on her body because the smell in the room was overpowering. She added that the girl's frame was mis-shapen, with one hip higher than the other and her skirt likely padded to disguise it. In the armed camp of Frederick William's wife and daughters and with the king utterly charmed by this simple creature who showed so little that she knew her place, his womenfolk took pains to smear her image. It seemed their own future positions were now at stake, and having been raised in an atmosphere of spite they reacted in the same vein.

---

[11] écu's and florins were roughly half the value of a Wolfenbüttel thaler in the 18th century.

[12] Antonia Fraser, <u>Marie Antoinette</u> (New York: Anchor Books, 2002), 42. The écu's value is commensurate with the florin. Elisabeth's 20,000 thaler dowry is c. 65 % smaller than Marie Antoinette's.

[13] Fraser, 43.

Field Marshall Grumbkow, Frederick William's Foreign Minister and crony, tried to overcome the campaign against Elisabeth by telling Fritz what his own daughter Jetta had observed in 1730:

> When she [Elisabeth] appears in front of her mother, she does not open her mouth and blushes every time one talks to her. This derives from being brought up very strictly, not enjoying any freedom, not receiving ladies in her room . . . I who had the honor to talk to her during the masked ball, where she was alone and undisturbed, I can assure you that there is in her no lack neither of intelligence nor judgment and that her behavior is reasonable, that she has compassion and seemed to be of very good natural disposition.[14]

Grumbkow had already benefitted financially from the Wolfenbüttel connection, receiving a finding fee of forty thousand thalers and negotiating the marriage, from a grateful Austrian government.[15] His hovering presence over both the King and Crown Prince was accepted by both of them, on the King's part by political necessity and on Fritz's by his recurring financial crises. He constantly needed a bailout and those who hoped for his aid in the future themselves, namely the Junkers, landed aristocrats of the district, and friends in Berlin, contributed regularly; it was a down payment on their future. A partnership of minds between the monarch and his heir would have avoided Seckendorff and Grumbkow's manipulations, but until the last months of Frederick William's life he and his son were a combination of sodium violently reacting with water, neither one willing nor able to trust the other.

When Fritz had met Elisabeth himself, he said his fiancée was pretty with delicate features, but had no breeding and dressed very badly. That she was taller than himself[16] he did not mention. She was, after all, the daughter of a man of "giant-like stature . . . known as the tallest prince in Germany."[17] Fritz at 1.63 meters (roughly 5' 4") was acutely aware of how they would appear as a couple and must have found it annoying.[18]

---

[14] Noack, 43.   [15] Noack, 28.   [16] Noack, 48.   [17] Noack, 14.

[18] Günther Rieger, Elisabeth Christine Gattin Friedrichs II von Preussen, (Nördlingen: Druckerei Steinmeier, 1999), 2. The engraving of their wedding 12 June 1733 by Georg Friedrich Schmidt clearly shows Elisabeth nearly half a head taller than Fritz; on page 40 a woodcut shows the couple observing their golden wedding anniversary. Fritz is the shorter of the two.

Disappointed in her lack of spirit, he wished she could spend time with her grandmother, the ambitious and pushy Duchess of Brunswick, who might be able to energize the unworldly princess.

Fritz's fear of boredom seemed to concern him more than anything else, but nothing would have been grounds for rejecting her. Elisabeth had made the grade with his father, who would carry the union forward no matter what. Proving just that point, Fritz's acceptance of the marriage promoted him in rank to a colonelcy in command of the Goltz Regiment, newly headquartered at Ruppin some thirty-five miles (55 km) north of Berlin.

Above everything, his bride's appearance and bearing mattered far less than his determination to get out from under his father's control. Princes as well as princesses were everywhere slaves to their parents until they married. Frederick William held all the cards and Fritz must play the game to its end. If marriage was the strategy, so be it. His father had laid down the rules of play in February of 1732: once a son was produced, Fritz could travel outside Prussia. Freedom was going to cost him and the choke chain would be tight as long as his father was alive.

He bared his contempt before Seckendorff in a letter: "I shall (once married) let Madame go her ways and as far as I am concerned I shall do as I please. And long live freedom!"[19] To Grumbkow after his initial suicide threat about being "tied to a fool"[20] he was milder: "I am sorry for the poor girl. There is going to be one more unhappy princess in the world."[21] More openly he admitted to Wilhelmine, "I do not hate her so much as I pretend. I affect complete dislike, so that the King may value my obedience all the more."[22] Checkmate!

The King ignored Fritz's grumblings since he already knew about a promising connection in the late summer of 1731, before his betrothal. Beautiful, blond haired Luise Eleonore of Wreech, four years older than young Fritz and ten years younger than her husband (and the mother of his five children) had made a deep and lyrical impression on nineteen

---

[19] Walter Henry Nelson, <u>The Soldier Kings The House of Hohenzollern</u> (New York: G.P. Putnam's Sons, 1970) 137.

[20] Constance Wright, <u>A Royal Affinity The Story of Frederick the Great and His Sister Wilhelmina of Bayreuth</u>. (New York: Charles Scribner's Sons, 1965) 147.

[21] Nelson, 137-138.

[22] Nelson, 137-138.

year old Fritz, who wrote a poem to her with the dedication: "A subject cannot carry greater reverence than what I have in my heart for you."[23] Whether he made a physical impression on her as well was never determined. But Eleonore became pregnant in September not long after their first meeting and the child, born the following May of 1732, was assumed by many to be Fritz's child.[24]

Like many reigning sovereigns before him and since, Frederick William was told about his son's elaborate attentions to Frau von Wreech and their possible result. ". . . the King hopes that the Crown Prince will do the same to the Bevern," Grumbkow informed Seckendorff in August. Considering the Byzantine workings of his son's mind by the age of 19, it is well within reason that Fritz counted on his father's pleasure all along. He would not have been the first.

By autumn Fritz had come to terms with his fate and wrote to Grumbkow:

> Marriage brings one to full age and as soon as I will be that I will also be the master of my house and my wife will have nothing to say. Simply, no woman in the administration, for nothing in the world.

Later he added:

> Concerning my wedding, it will be happening, if my father is alive, if not, I shall slowly keep my word, but keep (it) I will.[25]

He was as good as his word.

Elisabeth's reaction is strikingly different. In the same month as her marriage she writes of happiness and contentment in her new state and the affection being extended to her by the king and the rest of the royal

---

[23] Noack, 66.

[24] Nancy Mitford. Frederick the Great (New York: Harper & Row, 1970) 221. Some twenty-six years later near the end of the Seven Years War Fritz again saw the palace at Tamsel where he had met and attended on this early love. The fortunes of war between Prussia and Russia had left it smashed and despoiled, reportedly with the macabre corpse of a mutilated woman lying at its entrance. Eleonore having already fled to Berlin Fritz, to his credit, sent her a small sum. Facing the harsh reality of ruinous war costs Fritz reported himself only able to respond to her subsequent pleading letters with personal regrets but no more cash. "We are all in the same case."

[25] Noack, 58.

family. Naïveté may have been behind her words, but a desire to accept her husband and her situation is equally possible. His past adventures as well as his desperate escape, would not necessarily have come to her ears. A sheltered youth makes her optimism appear quite natural. Also, Elisabeth had an advocate at the court of Berlin, but it was the one person guaranteed to inflame her bridegroom, his father the king. Words of praise from that quarter would only further corrode whatever grudging appreciation of his wife might come into Fritz's mind.

Bitterness had poisoned him years before, by a childhood of physical and mental abuse culminating in the trauma of watching his friend Katte's head being cut off at Küstrin, probably the most traumatic lesson a father could impose. Harsh discipline was expected from a king's hand, but in Frederick William's case harsh discipline was not enough. Either inspired by the work of his grandfather, the Great Elector, or sickened by the extravagant excess of his father, the hunchback who worshipped the elegance of Versailles, Frederick William was determined to jam a well-rounded, intelligent heir into the square peg hole of Prussian militarism and austerity. Intellectual curiosity and liberalism must not stand in the way of proper rule of the state, which the king had rescued from his own father's misrule. Spare the rod, and the humiliation, and spoil the child was holy writ to this thoroughly confounded father.

In almost every way Fritz and Elisabeth's whole married life was tied to the climactic events at Küstrin in November of 1730. His father had utterly defeated him and from those bitter days on he knew that only marriage and the siring of an heir would signal the beginning of any life of his own making. That view led him to the altar, but it allowed no room in his heart for a girl who was his father's candidate and protégé. No matter how steadfast Elisabeth's loyalty would endure over their fifty-three years of marriage, for him she remained as he saw her at the beginning, the ransom for his emancipation. Sadly, for her it was a mirage, and a hurtful one.

CHAPTER FOUR

IN NAME ALONE

The round peg's final seating into the square hole of marriage was almost at hand. All his life Fritz had been conditioned to accept harsh sentences with little praise for his effort. By this time he accepted his father's mandate: Elisabeth was a perfect fit for a Hohenzollern bride, politically and morally. No argument would alter that. Once in the bedroom, however, and behind a closed door, the marriage bed would be something else. Fritz had no intention of begetting heirs, no matter what demands or bribes were laid down. He would simply dissemble his way out of them.

The king and queen traveled from Berlin separately, no doubt to spare their ears from each other's sniping, joining each other at Helmstedt,[1] three days before the wedding. Bumped and bruised from a 150 mile trip in large "Berlin" travel coaches on roads well below the standards of France or England, Frederick William had enough breath left to greet his wife as "Mein Fiekchen,"[2] my little fuck, a pointed salute from his own coarse nature to level hers. They and other guests coming from afar spent the following day resting and recovering from the very real pains of travel. Sophia Dorothea would have added his crude words to the sharp thorns already in her side from frustration over the failure of her matchmaking. There was little to celebrate, to her mind, about a son's union with a tongue-tied, nervously giggling minor princess. He should have been offered a better candidate!

The Brunswick-Wolfenbüttels put on a brave show at the Salzdahlum[3] wedding ceremony on 12 June 1733, heralded by trumpet fanfares, drum rolls and twenty-four gun salute and presided over by Elisabeth's confessor Abbot Dreissigmark, a name cryptically prophetic.[4]

---

[1] Helmstedt, 25 miles (40 km.) east of Salzdahlum, at the western end of the Cold War's "Berlin Access Road."

[2] Friedrich Ludwig Müller, "Elisabeth Christine - Königen von Preußen (II) *Der schöne Schein*, <u>Monumente</u> 7/8 (1999): 61.

[3] Since its construction 50 years earlier it had not yet shown the gradual decay that led to its dismantling a century later. Almost nothing of it remains now.

[4] The literal translation of "Dreissigmark," thirty mark, ominously recalls the payment Judas Iscariot received for betraying Jesus Christ.

The wedding feast followed in the new banqueting hall with an orgy of choices between veal, venison, lobster, crab, trout and salmon set before guests on golden plates brought from the Schloss at Wolfenbüttel. Dancing and dramas by the court staff entertained the guests afterwards. Lavish display was expected by the Hohenzollerns from a family whose daughter was elevated and blessed to become the crown princess of Prussia. Ferdinand Albrecht's stressed treasury never fully recovered.

Besides the dowry of 25,000 thalers her father had to dig deeper for another 35,000 for the wedding itself and yet more to polish up Salzdahlum and attach the new banqueting hall. Since both Elisabeth and her brother Karl would marry within three weeks of each other, a double wedding could have saved Wolfenbüttel thalers but was never considered. Sharing a Crown Prince's limelight was unthinkable.

Considering his marriage an act of state was the only way Fritz could stomach the thought - that and his father's pressure. His grandiose expectations of a throng of high level guests were let down hard; only the setting itself was impressive. Ferdinand Albrecht had a hard landing of his own, expecting that his wife's sister in Vienna would chip in with the cost, but no money ever came. Fritz may have known about that too, more wormwood and gall bathing his ego.

When the vows and prayers of blessing, the feasting, toasting and romantic gaiety wound down, Elisabeth and Fritz went off to their Hochzeit Nacht (wedding night) where they passed a scant half hour alone together before Fritz left her to chat with wedding guests in Salzdahlum's gardens. What was said and done during those few minutes alone is not known. Elisabeth left no account about either her new husband's words or his sufficiency and it never suited Fritz to explain his haste. However, his relief was obvious late that night when he wrote to Wilhelmine of thanking God it was over, adding "I am wholly yours . . . Adieu, Frederick."[5]

It is tempting to wish that Fritz might have hinted to his bride that the strategy of grudging submission to his father's marriage command in no way included his fulfilling physical obligations to her. Elisabeth's forbearance and outward loyalty over the years of their marriage would

---

[5] Ludwig Reiners, <u>Frederick the Great A Biography</u> (New York: Putnam, 1960), 68.

then be easier to square with the treatment he meted out to her. But cold reality gives no good odds for egoism being overruled by his highly touted enlightened mind. No husband of their century would make such a confession to his wife. Fritz's well developed double nature allowed him to endure his father's stranglehold and accept Seckendorf's and Grumbkow's assurance that Vienna would pay the debts Frederick William was not aware of until such time as he could direct his own affairs without interference from anyone.

For an individual content to operate on the other guy's money, why should he contribute anything toward Elisabeth's understanding of his motives. Most likely she was simply an expressway to his goal, autonomy. Elisabeth received short shrift from his pen and his words after that. He had clearly resolved to wring out any warmth from their day, and contemptuously bragged about it to Wilhelmine.

He was still pouting during Elisabeth's family's farewell dinner in the Kleines Schloss three days later. The food again was elegant with Portuguese oranges, Hamburg lobster, crab and salmon and Braunschweig venison and veal washed down the gullet with French champagne and wine from Spain, but only his parents and siblings qualified as "royals." Dancing came afterward but Fritz complained of stomach cramps, escaping the undistinguished company and grumbling later that no one of any significance was there. That this last family evening in her childhood home would be a treasured memory for his bride probably was lost on Fritz. If it occured to him at all he would have thought she was too dull to notice the snub. Even a visit he made to Wolfenbüttel's renowned library went unremarked; neither his wife nor her family gained any intellectual points in spite of the all too obvious contrast with his family's no-frills practicality. He had been sold short and nothing would alter his mind. Resentment hardened into resolve: a marriage had been made but it would contain neither cold mating nor inflamed anger; simply no attachment and, of course, no children ever.

He and his bride left for Berlin the following day, welcoming crowds cheering them all along the way and Elisabeth pleasing everyone with waves and winks. Her fresh eighteen year old enthusiasm was contagious and from a distance, all appeared to be well. They stayed briefly at Charlottenburg, then just outside the city, until their formal entrance on 17 June through the city gate at Köpenick escorted by a showy procession of sixty carriages, each drawn by six horses. Berliners began gathering at 3 am that morning to get a look at their new Crown Princess.

Less than a week later the other bride and groom were married, a different union altogether. Seven sons and six daughters were eventually born to Karl and Philippine Charlotte. Elisabeth, watching this couple declare their vows, might have thought that surely her Fritz would set aside his bitter pride long enough to give her some sign of closeness. Instead she got detached correctness all through their honeymoon summer and beyond, and he kept on writing to Wilhelmine as if he remained "wholly" hers.

On the heels of the later wedding, Fritz was ordered back to his regiment at Ruppin while Elisabeth stayed behind in the newly remodeled Crown Prince's Palace on Unter den Linden near the Royal Palace itself. Built in the previous century and lived in by a member of the Court staff, the king thought it was very well suited to his son's new status, a prospective pater familias. But for Elisabeth it was foreboding, unfamiliar territory; all too soon her days descended into indifferent neglect. In those times a woman's life operated at the sufferance of her husband with no position of her own except at his side. Members of the royal court took their cue from the higher positioned person in a marriage. Because of their snobbery every friction and callous behavior toward the lesser party was noted and they sniffed the wind to behave accordingly.

She could not have the comfort of even a short visit with her parents. Today, a visit home is usually the best cure for post-adolescent homesickness. But before the modern age travel was a major barrier, and in Elisabeth's case suitable arrangements had to square with her new royal state. A year and a half passed before she got permission to visit her parents and her childhood home. It turned out to be a precious time that renewed her spirit. Compared to Berlin, life in the Kleines Schloss was simple and intimate, and "home." Although her mother was ill that January, Elisabeth's presence lightened the days and after her departure her mother wrote that she was feeling much better.

Less than two months later such a renewal would no longer have been possible. Her grandfather, Duke Ludwig Rudolf of Brunswick-Wolfenbüttel died and her father Ferdinand Albrecht succeeded to the title and moved across the moat to the palace. Elisabeth had come just in time with fond grandparents, parents and siblings still there to gather her back into the fold. Returning to Berlin was a harsh contrast. Her father had sent her off with the good advice of sticking closely to Fritz's interests and ambitions. The Hohenzollerns were too full of contradictions and frustrated egos for an outsider to satisfy. Besides, Elisabeth basically was only a Pre-Queen whose future was not yet certain. For her there was no light at the end of a lonely tunnel, nor even a tunnel at all. Serving her husband's plans was the only sure-footed path.

Life in Wolfenbüttel had never been austere or demanding enough to prepare her for Berlin and its high-powered ruling family as well as its haughty nobility, but as long as Frederick William was alive Elisabeth would have a protector. He might not be able to change his wife's dislike or the family gossip she encouraged. However, his servants and subjects knew that slights and omissions of respect to Elisabeth could bring down the king's formidable wrath against them. Her father was known as a respected leader in the Austrian army and honored as such by the king.

Ferdinand Albrecht was well aware of what had led up to his daughter's wedding and its aftermath. The advice he sent with her back to Berlin pointed her way around royal gossip. Fritz knew from the beginning that he must tread lightly with her, but once his father was gone, he would be free to make use of her when necessary and shove her away when not. For the four years before his father's death he only kept her personally involved when he needed her brother's troops. Otherwise she was sidelined.

A minefield opened for Elisabeth in the beginning, with Fritz a four day's journey away and in no way inclined to smooth her path from afar. Mother-in-law and sisters-in-law stood back, waiting expectantly for her to put a foot wrong. Frederick William's approval was bitter enough for the family to swallow, but then he added 25,000 thalers of his own to her dowry in order to help pay for a country retreat for the newlyweds. At that their spite hardened and was given free reign after he departed Berlin within days of his son leaving for Ruppin, to inspect his state and beloved army. Separation of wife from husband was hardly unexpected in light of Fritz's past errors. Coming to terms with his father's demands must now be carried forward by serious application to his regiment. He was not out of the woods yet and he knew it.

Had Hohenzollern tradition and pride been able to step ahead into the future and see the practicalities, they might have recognized that Elisabeth's unpretentious childhood in the Kleines Schloss prepared her far better for a military officer's quarters in Ruppin than the lonely rooms of a Berlin palace. With her open and accepting nature, living closely side by side with her mate, she could have blossomed in spite of Fritz's prickly nature. However, the days of baroque stage-settings and royal-blooded high life were still in full flower. Even though the king wanted a pregnancy as soon as possible, he was bound by the conventional wisdom that his son's quarters at Ruppin would not do for a Crown Princess and her household. Fritz was delighted to agree. He could ignore his bride without needing to know her. Whatever Elisabeth might be owed for throwing open his gilded cage, she would have to swipe off to profit and loss. He was not going to be ruled by a wife's needs and not much longer by a father's.

The hope that Elisabeth's mother might warn her about Fritz's mother and sisters is not supported by any evidence. All the same, Antoinette Amalia must have known something of the family dynamics in Berlin beyond the political currents ebbing and flowing between Hohenzollern, Habsburg and Hannover. There were too many webs of intrigue in the intermarriages of the royal mob.[6] The grim aspect of Sophia Dorothea's parents' marriage, broken during her early childhood and her mother's lifelong exile, was a well-known tragedy. Some mention must have been made of the challenges ahead for Elisabeth. About the only saving grace fate provided in that summer of 1733 was the absence of Wilhelmine, Fritz's childhood confidant and ally. Now the princess of Bayreuth, Wilhelmine was living there with her husband and infant daughter.

During holidays and other family celebrations Fritz returned to Berlin off and on, usually staying where his wife lodged in the Crown Prince's palace in Berlin. But Elisabeth learned early on that her husband's time and presence were his own to give, and her place in the royal pecking order was far below his family. Fritz vowed that any queen of his would live in isolation. To eat his words now was beyond him. Elisabeth came

---

[6] Queen Victoria's 19th century description of her relatives in England and across the Continent.

from a positive life, in spite of its lack of pretension. His nature had been laced with a cynic's view.

Probably the most blistering example of this was his heartless comment on his father-in-law's death in a letter written to Wilhelmine fifteen months after his marriage. Ferdinand Albrecht's long period of waiting to become Duke of Brunswick-Wolfenbüttel had been followed by his untimely death only six months later.

> My God, I am charmed by the Duke of Brunswick's conduct; he has had the good manners to die like a man of honor to please his son. I consider that he has not misused worldly grandeur."[7]

The not-so-thinly veiled dig at Frederick William was obvious, and compounded when Fritz wrote to his father for permission to go to Berlin and console his bride. It reeks of bilious mockery. Perhaps his visit helped her, in the short run at least, but true to form, he returned to Ruppin and the regiment soon after.

Without her husband Elisabeth drifted into a banal routine of writing homesick letters in the mornings and visiting back and forth with women of Berlin society in the afternoons as social protocol demanded. Nights were long and sleep elusive. In deference to her son's position, Sophia Dorothea grudgingly accepted her daughter-in-law's timid efforts to fit in, but without warmth or compassion. Too many scalds from the past shrouded her efforts. She would not smooth the path of this rising star whose virtues her husband trumpeted to everyone. She also knew, as every queen must, that Elisabeth's place at court would outshine hers once there was an heir. Her daughters followed her lead, assured of their brother's indifference to his wife. There was no one beyond her own household who could bind up her wounds; Elisabeth must find her own way.

Frederick William had other concerns. Now his heir had accepted a well brought up and mild consort, his wife had swallowed defeat and his children remained afraid of him. What more could a dyspeptic despot wish for? Accomplishing all that, he turned to drilling his Lange Kerle, a regiment of giants, and relaxing in the evenings with his cronies over tobacco and liquor.

---

[7] Pierre Gaxotte, <u>Frederick *the Great*</u> (New Haven: Yale University Press, 1942), 117.

CHAPTER FIVE

RHEINSBERG'S PROMISE, REMUSBERG REALITY

In Ruppin that autumn, and of age at last in his father's eyes, the air of freedom had never been sweeter to Fritz. Thinking back to the price he had paid for it, from Küstrin, to Wolfenbüttel and back again, he was well content. Elisabeth living without him in Berlin, was getting used to court life as well as to his family. Being on her own there was probably best; his presence would have complicated if not compromised her progress. His father had eased off nagging about an heir and the huff he had affected over their lackluster wedding began to fade. For the first time in years he was nearly happy.

Elisabeth put on a smiling face to write home some weeks later like the dutiful daughter she was,

> . . . I cannot be anything but happy . . . and if it remains the same as the beginning, I shall at all times be happily content. The King, the Queen and the whole Royal Family are extending to me so much love and friendship . . .[1]

Valiant words, but life in Wolfenbüttel, even in the Kleines Schloss, was no preparation for Berlin and a palace. None of the family except her father-in-law offered her real friendship and no baby would be coming along to distract her from cold reality. Only Frau von Katsch was there to help Elisabeth out from under her shyness. Katsch may have seemed small town and provincial to the court, but Elisabeth needed someone who understood her, whether the arrogance of Berlin society stomached it or not.[2]

Entertaining ladies of the nobility was a daunting task, but meeting their expectations was the bellwether to measure her success as a Crown Princess. She had to endure it. Her shy gawkiness, possibly even the secret, or not so secret, failed coupling of her wedding night all could be passed around sooner or later. Juicy gossip was as irresistible

---

[1] Paul Noack, Elisabeth Christine und Friedrich der Grosse: ein Frauenleben in Preussen (Stuttgart: Klett-Cotta, 2001), 59.
[2] Robert B. Asprey, Frederick the Great The Magnificent Enigma, (New York: Ticknor & Fields, 1986), 112.

then as always. A new persona was upon her, not any longer simply her parents' daughter but the most important daughter in Prussia, and now she must cope with the public face of her position. The fact was that she had been dealt a losing hand: husband delighted to escape, mother-in-law and siblings-in-law waiting to pounce. The only friend she had, besides Katsch, was Frederick William. From the beginning he had been fond of her and she reached out to him gratefully, providing table treats from home like Brunswick rotwurst and Wolfenbüttel's strong Mumme beer, both forbidden fruit to his chronically stressed gut. But in spite of the gastric horrors they brought on, her gifts brought the two of them even closer. She seemed to empathize with his self-indulgent compulsions, something his family could only criticize. A straightforward personality herself, they could appreciate each other. His favor to her was obvious enough to the family when in August he gave her the use of a small country residence, today's Schönhausen, ten miles (16 km.) from the crowded center of Berlin, where she could live with her own household during Fritz's summer absences and escape the heat of the city.

By the next summer, Fritz was even farther and longer away. After four months of pleading, by Elisabeth and himself, his father finally agreed to let him join Prussian troops going to the aid of Austria in the War of the Polish Succession. Just before the wedding at Salzdahlum Augustus the Strong, the prodigiously alcoholic king of Poland had died, starting a continent wide spat about who should sit on his vacant throne. France and Austria each proposed candidates, and Russia joined Austria's side along with Prussia to form an army led by the famed Eugene of Savoy, considered the best military leader in Europe.

Fritz was starry-eyed at the chance to stand at Eugene's feet and learn how to lead. To plead his case he turned to his wife; her simple soul would welcome any chance to reconcile husband and father and in May she obliged, writing to the King:

> I believe that this would be for him the greatest of all joys,
> because it is very natural that a young man would like to
> view something like that and especially a Crown Prince,
> who is ambitious and whose profession is War.[3]

---

[3] Noack, 70.

By the end of June 1734 the Emperor's troops had a new junior officer. Yet again, living together could be deferred. Her effort received little thanks and simply pushed her farther into the sidelines.

Elisabeth's father saw the pitfalls she must avoid, wanting to:

> . . . give you the guiding principle to strengthen your influence to only interfere in [Fritz's] affairs when he wishes it . . . . [. . . never confide in the Queen] as it seems to me that the future King [Fritz] has no intention that his mother should have a great [role] in his reign.[4]

Ferdinand Albrecht hit the nail on the head here about his son-in-law; in the event Sophia Dorothea received kind words but no influence once her son was king.

As summer ended news came that Frederick William had suffered a massive stroke. Unmoved at first, Fritz dawdled along, writing to his sister Wilhelmine:

> I have decided to console myself with whatever happens, for after all I am strongly convinced that during his lifetime I will have only a slim chance for happiness.[5]

But his self-pity was jolted awake when his mother sent a courier to Bayreuth in early October, telling Wilhelmine and Fritz who was visiting her that the King was dying. Finally the prodigal son hurried to his father's bedside.

What he found was sobering - a grotesquely swollen stomach and legs, dropsical genitals that prevented urination and labored breathing due to fluid gathering in the lungs. However, this man was a gritty survivor who turned his face away from defeat and hung on like a stoic, gradually recovering after months of awful suffering. Gout, asthma, surgery to drain away quarts of fluid from his legs were all endured and finally, confoundingly, overcome. In modern terms Frederick William proved himself a tough old bird, and by the beginning of 1735 he was back at business in Berlin and Fritz was back in Ruppin.

The autumn crisis left a nagging unease in Fritz's mind of what was coming; ". . . make good use of my mistakes . . . .[6] his father had warned.

---

[4] Noack, 72. Sophia Dorothea remained higher on her son's list than his wife.
[5] Asprey, 101.
[6] Asprey, 102.

In a few months that warning was verified when France and Austria settled the Polish succession between them, leaving Prussia out entirely. Frederick William had been promised that his legal claims to territories adjoining Cologne on the Rhine river would be part of the peace settlement if Prussian troops fought for Austria. He saw that he had been swindled and (pointing to his eldest son), told the Austrian envoy in Berlin "here is one who will avenge me."[7] He would and in time he did, in spades!

Shortly after Fritz's marriage the King had suggested that he look for an estate in the vicinity of Ruppin which could be shared with Elisabeth. Probably thoughts of an heir prompted Frederick William to buy it with Elisabeth's dowry and funds of his own. Excited at the prospect, Fritz had found within months the old domain of Rheinsberg, fifteen miles (24 km.) northeast of Ruppin. There was a beautifully situated but remote and rundown castle on the Grienerick See, a small lake surrounded by woods and farms. In November of 1733 Frederick William bought the property with 50,000 thalers of his own money, and the balance of 25,000 thalers from Elisabeth's dowry.

It was an investment in their future family. Fritz could hone his military and management skills at Ruppin, and Elisabeth would join him in their own home when it was ready. Restoration was long overdue for the dilapidated castle but Frederick William figured that Fritz's agreement to begin a true married life was worth the money needed to pave village streets and market place, plaster the houses and tile the roofs. Prosperity would certainly follow when a crown prince and princess and a hoped for brood of children, preferably sons, lived there. These plans of the father did not match the plan of the son, but Fritz kept his mouth shut and bided his time.

Rheinsberg is something of a paradise of the north, located on the edge of the Mecklenburg Lake Plateau, still today a traveler's destination for enjoying the lakes, quiet inlets and water wanderings. One of Fritz's mid-twentieth century biographers lyrically described it:

> . . . an immense watery waste, gray and green, lightly
> touched with mist; with soft sand which sank beneath the
> feet, tall grasses yellow and sharp as swords, silver birches,

---

[7] Asprey, 10.

beeches, green and black pines which endured the squalls
of autumn stoically, pools stretching on forever . . . at close
of day, when the rim of the horizon was like burnished cop-
per, the waters purpled and the tree tops were tinged with
glowing reflections.[8]

Remodeling began in March of 1734 with instructions to the builder
not to make a silk purse out of a sow's ear. Inhabitants of the town even
received some tax relief to put the new lord of the manor in a favorable
light.[9] Frederick William was leaving no stone unturned. Fritz was eager
to imprint his own style on the building. His close friend and fellow
officer Georg von Knobelsdorff knew what he was after and designed
that spirit into Fritz and Elisabeth's first, and last, home of their own.[10]
The transformation from decayed walls to delicately appointed rooms
proved Fritz's exquisite taste.

They would come into their own in the Rheinsberg years. He with a
personal "university" where he could bury himself in long days of reading and study, often starting at four o'clock in the morning until noon
and after dinner until the early hours next day. He began writing letters to great minds across the continent, including the French Philosophe Voltaire, and also indulging his love affair with playing the flute,
both tastes his father detested. In all, Rheinsberg was his dream house
of kindred spirits. Even his wife, he admitted, would be a decoration
within it.

Less a goose, more a swan, Elisabeth arrived in mid-August of 1736.
Dancing lessons had relaxed her awkwardness, and language lessons
had improved her French - mandatory in Fritz's company. An eager pu-
pil, the tutoring and small successes had polished her. Berlin had been
purgative, but at the same time it had seasoned her as Wolfenbüttel
never would. Gaining the king's approval had overridden his wife and
daughters' fault-finding and brought Elisabeth closer to a new confidence in herself. The king's feelings were obvious enough to gall the

---

[8] Pierre Gaxotte, <u>Frederick the Great</u>. trans. R.A.Bell, (New Haven: Yale University Press, 1942), 121.

[9] Asprey, 98.

[10] Giles MacDonogh, <u>Frederick the Great *A Life in Deed and Letters*</u> (London: Phoenix Press, 2000), 107.

rest of the family, especially Fritz, but not enough to keep him from making good use of her high marks with his father. In his own judgment he was more important than any of them.

Another wife with more ambition and prestige might have reached at that time for a star turn, but such was not Elisabeth's nature. She was starting to care for Fritz and more than willing to shine only in his reflected glory. After just a few months together she was predicting that he would become "the Phoenix of our time"[11] and wrote to her grandmother that autumn:

> Truly, one can say: He is the Greatest Prince of our time, not only [as] a prince, but also as a contemporary. He is a scholar, possesses spirit, as much as one wants. He is fair, helpful, does not want to harm anyone, is magnanimous, . . . temperate, does not love dissipation, not with wine nor anywhere else. His heart is in the right place.[12]

Warming to a grandmother's heart, such extravagant praise showed that Elisabeth had shed her timidity and believed their real life together was beginning at last. Fritz appeared to give her a wife's place instead of pushing her aside like the necessary evil and object of ridicule she had been in Berlin. Hope must have soared.

The hound stayed at her back though, to be seen in the same letter,

> The Empress (her aunt and namesake in Vienna) made me the honor of notifying me about the pregnancy of Madame la Duchess de Lorraine [Maria Theresia] and she wrote . . . that she ought to be in fairly good health for her state. That is a child that is worth more than a thousand children who are born . . .[13]

Her cousin, Maria Theresia, eighteen months younger than herself and only three months in a marriage bed, was pregnant with her first child. Such things mattered to a grandmother and much more to an Empress. Reporting it to Elisabeth, three years married and only a few weeks in

---

[11] Noack, 77.

[12] Noack, 73.

[13] Elisabeth Christine Letters, Niedersächsisches Landesarchiv - Staatsarchiv Wolfenbüttel, 1Alt 24 Nr. 287 Seite 027-028. n.d.

residence with her husband in Rheinsberg, was family news soaked in disapproval. Elisabeth wrote back with an upbeat description of days and nights at Rheinsberg where she was in marvelous condition. In the event, her cousin's first child turned out to be a girl who lived only four months. The next two offspring were also daughters, one dying within a year and the other spending her twenty-eight years of life in a convent in Prague, proving yet again that first starters out of the maternity gate did not always get into the winner's circle.[14]

Fritz was less uptight than he would be ever again. His father's orders had been obeyed; a safe haven had been reached where his mind and spirit could be filled to the brim before the weight of the crown descended. His father was only forty-eight. Self-indulgence at the table stirred with a short fuse, had abused his digestion and often brought him down but he always rebounded in fairly short order, walking away from a sickbed robust and combative. Health crises followed by extraordinary recoveries had long since desensitized family and ministers to his screams and shrieks.

Fritz's did not have to worry about all that yet. In the meantime he would dig into the meat of ruling, military strategy and history that he had been denied at home. Telling Elisabeth he did not wish for his father's death and indeed would feel more sadness than many who pretended loyalty while he lived,[15] at the same time he realized how badly his world view had been stunted by Frederick William's stubborn refusal to keep in depth study of world affairs out of his reach. That was the past, now at Rheinsberg he called the shots and set the studies. Once he became king he was going to rule decisively and rationally, no matter the cost to anyone, anywhere.

The short tether he wore after Küstrin allowed no travel outside Prussia, but new comrades could now travel to him. Forbidden books could be bought and delivered to his tower library. He gathered men to live at Rheinsberg who were known quantities: Georg Wenzeslas von Knobelsdorff, who had remodeled the building and setting, Dietrich, Freiherr von Keyserlingk who Fritz had named Césarion and his best

---

[14] Franz Weihrich, <u>Stammtafel zur Geschichte des Hauses Habsburg</u> (Prag: Buchhändler der Kaiserlichen Academie der Wissenschaften in Wien, 1892)
[15] Noack, 74.

friend,[16] Isaac François Egmont de Chasot, a nineteen year old flute player, and Charles Etienne Jordan, Fritz's guru on the cultural world he had not seen for himself. Others joined the circle from time to time, Fritz noted they never sat down to dinner under twenty-two or more. As Rheinsberg's academy came together Fritz decided that Elisabeth had made enough progress to join them. She must have an appointed place or else his father would never believe that orders to get an heir were being followed. One of the first shipments from Berlin was a king-sized marriage bed, a practical if not very subtle, reminder of the prime directive.

Fritz observed that the women fit very well into his stage-setting life.

> Now that the sex has come here the place seems to take on a new brilliance from them; the conversation is more lively and our pleasure is more radiant.[17]

"Brilliance" and "radiance" must serve as he fades her into the group. Though he was to write numerous poems to other women during the rest of his life, he never dedicated any to her, even while they lived side by side at Rheinsberg. Antoine Pesne's portrait of 1738 shows her grown into elegant beauty and Fritz's middle class friend Jakob Bielfeld describes her explicitly.

> She is tall and grown up perfectly well. I have never seen such an even waist in all its dimensions. Her breasts, her hands and her feet could serve as models for a painter. She has a very delicate complexion and large blue eyes in which liveliness and tenderness vie for superiority which gives her look something of an ingeniousness. She has an open forehead, well placed eyebrows, a small and somewhat pointed but well-formed nose, a pleasant mouth, red lips, and her chin is, as well as her neck, charming. Her face speaks of goodness and one can truly say that her whole stature has been formed by the hands of the Muses.[18]

---

[16] Gaxotte, 125. (Césarion was the name, in French of course, of Julius Caesar and Cleopatra's son.)

[17] Gaxotte, 130.

[18] Noack, 86-87.

Remodeling at the castle was not finished that August when Elisabeth arrived. A steady hand was badly needed to deal with the tangle of conflicting claims between the village magistrate and the castle. At Elisabeth's suggestion Wilhelm von Rohwedel, who had been with Fritz in Küstrin and Ruppin, was appointed to bring order out of chaos. Ultimately successful in establishing who was actual owner and master, he would have little success in securing fiscal stability. Riding herd on Fritz's spending was impossible. Deep pockets had always been open for the picking when future preferment was at stake. For both donor and receiver it was acceptable practice. There was, in any case, no way the town of Rheinsberg, with only 700 people, could ever produce enough cash to support Fritz's needs.

Building materials were strewn around the courtyard and the servants' quarters were not completed, but the rubble had been swept up and the whole place looked an oasis of welcome as Fritz led Elisabeth through their apartments, seven rooms for him and five for her. Knobelsdorff had created a large, open living space in the south tower that was filled with light. Here, surely, was freedom and release from the tension in Berlin that stifled them both. Delicate white, green and gold walls ornamented the formal entrance hall opening onto Elisabeth's quarters. There were large portraits of her parents and soon there would be a painting of herself on the ceiling, primed now with white to prepare for it.

The bedroom suite contained few accessories besides a lacquered leather screen set in front of Elisabeth's mirrored-door armoire, a gift from Wolfenbüttel. Blue satin walls, gold tapestries and gold lace-bordered curtains set off the most impressive and important piece in the room, its huge Ehebett.[19] Separate sleeping rooms were the rule in stately lives of that era; Elisabeth actually slept in a small bed in a corner against one wall. Aside from this concession to reality, the main thought in Elisabeth's mind as Fritz showed her where they would live together, was that at last she seemed to be accepted by the man who had pledged his life to her.

Was the marriage bed ever in use by them both? Fritz tried to say

---

[19] Marriage bed.

that it was, that Elisabeth could not complain that he never slept with her nor could he explain why there was no child.[20] Fritz must have skated over the issue enough for his father to settle another 40,000 thalers of Fritz's overdue bills.[21] It could not come soon enough. Elisabeth's Frau von Katsch and two maids of honor had come with her as well as Augustin Deschamps, her reader and special tutor. Not long after the new court was assembled in September the king and queen visited them. Fritz and Elisabeth were glowing and everything pleased the king; it might turn out well after all.

Not everything was inspections and cold hard cash in those early months. There was romance as well in a local myth that placed one of the founders of Rome at Rheinsberg's gates. The legend intrigued Fritz since it paralleled his own flight from oppression. Romulus and Remus, the story ran, after weaned from the she-wolf, quarreled and Romulus came out the victor. However, Remus survived and supposedly fled 800 miles (1,280 km.) north to Rheinsberg, of all places, where he settled on an island in the Grienerick See.[22] The story mesmerized Fritz and from then on Rheinsberg was Remusberg.[23] Elisabeth caught the spirit and wrote to her mother:

> Those who seek for art, true and clear philosophy, and wit should come here: they will find everything in a state of perfection, as our master is in control of it all.[24]

Remusberg housed Fritz's love affair with everything French: paintings on the walls and music in the evenings, Fritz performing on his flute. His family, except for the king and queen, must wait for an invitation to visit. Elisabeth described it to her mother:

> . . . I have never seen anyone work as hard as he does: from six in the morning until one o'clock he works at reading, philosophy, and all the other noble studies. Dinner lasts from half-past one until three o'clock. After that we drink

---

[20] Asprey, 14.

[21] Asprey, 14.

[22] Gaxotte, 131.

[23] Asprey, 113. He also called it "my Sans Souci" well before he built the palace of that name in Potsdam.

[24] Asprey, 132.

coffee till four and then he gets down to work again until seven in the evening. Next music begins and lasts till nine o'clock. Then he writes, comes to play cards, and we generally sup at half-past ten or eleven . . . . I can truthfully say that he is the greatest prince of our time. . . . he is the Phoenix and I am proud to be the wife of so great a prince who has so many good qualities. To know him is to love him . . . .[25]

Elisabeth was a girl to let her husband have his way. She had been raised in the Lutheran tradition of obedience, marital and civil, to higher authority. A husband that was also a prince, and a Crown Prince, was lord and master absolute. Innate integrity compelled her to be a loyal, obedient wife in the first place, but now she was in love with him. Fritz was honest enough to write that:

I would be the most vile man in the world to say I did not like her, for she is of the most gentle nature, docile, thoughtful, and agreeable, and does everything to please me.[26]

In fairness, he had tried to avoid marrying her, predicting that there would be one more unhappy princess in the world. Yet once the marriage happened he grasped her support, moral and financial, with both hands and bit by bit squeezed her into the spot he had occupied under his father. Like himself then, she would earn no credit for passively accepting it. He could only see her as boring and the irony of their situation never really occurred to him.

Luckily, Elisabeth became a student herself at Rheinsberg. Always a reader, she began on French literature so valued by her husband. Charles Jordan helped her, widening horizons and cultural view as well as improving her French conversation. Descriptions of his travels in France, England and Holland enthralled everyone including Elisabeth. Inspired, she ventured into historical and literary studies as well and could discuss them with Fritz. All of it bore fruit in the short term during their four years together at Rheinsberg, but an even greater harvest was to come in the longer term, forty years on.

---

[25] Asprey, 132.
[26] G. P. Gooch, <u>Frederick the Great The Ruler, the Writer, the Man</u> (New York: Dorset Press, 1947), 117.

With artists in residence she learned new painting and etching techniques. And letter writing continued, both to her family and often to Frederick William, describing their days. To the latter she aimed it all toward Fritz's benefit, encouraging her father-in-law to mellow out in dealings with his tetchy son. Getting to know and understand his father had greatly helped her understand and deal with Fritz's hot temper. Along with all the positive, Elisabeth was aware of their inevitable future, and knew this golden time would not go on forever. Once it was gone Fritz would dive headlong into a new life where she would have very little part. While they were still together she must keep him in the loop with her relatives. Fritz was always leery of her brother Karl's coziness with Vienna, a looming bugbear, so she tried to steer Karl and Wolfenbüttel in Prussia's direction. Karl was soon persuaded to borrow 19,000 thalers for Fritz's benefit from wealthy Brunswick families at her request, which ought to have soothed Fritz's suspicions. But in truth, she had become Fritz's cash cow and not just the instigator of better relations between her husband and brother. Remusberg's days and nights of grace and charming display cost money and could not have been paid for without her.

CHAPTER SIX
PASSING THE BATON

Elisabeth's last free summer at Rheinsberg was marked by Fritz's changed attitude toward Frederick William's projects in East Prussia. In July of 1739 he wrote of prosperous farms and growing towns that showed the benefits of actively recruiting Protestants who had been expelled from France and Jews from all parts of Europe to settle in the area. With their skills and independent spirit, backed by the king's money, the grungy work of land clearing and swamp draining was changing the Prussian landscape and pushing forward Prussia's prosperity as a result. Finally he was giving his father credit, bragging to Voltaire that his father had "colonized this desert and made it fertile and useful,"[1] praise indeed.

The turnaround, completely sincere or not, softened Frederick William to the extent that he gave Fritz his year old stud farm at Trakehnen in East Prussia. It was doing well, worth a good twelve thousand thalers a year and providing animals for the army, particularly the Goltz regiment. "Found Money" was always welcome but this included a new softening of his father's stiff opinions. While still enjoying the glow of approval Fritz wrote expansively, even unctuously to his wife,

I am anticipating with great impatience the moment when I can embrace you and can assure you that I am totally yours.[2]

nearly the same words he sent to Wilhelmine in 1733 following his unfruitful wedding night. In this case words died with the writing; *impatience to embrace* was never observed.

As in 1734 after her letters to Frederick William aided Fritz's entry into active army service he had written of how he appreciated and depended on her. But by 1739 her day with him had reached its afternoon. He had finished answering Machiavelli's The Prince with his own book, The Refutation of The Prince of Machiavelli. Fritz rejected out of

[1] Giles MacDonogh, Frederick the Great A Life in Deed and Letters, (London: Phoenix Press, 2000), 127.
[2] Paul Noack, Elisabeth Christine und Friedrich der Grosse und ein Frauenleben in Preussen, (Stuttgart: Klett-Cotta, 2001), 76.

hand Machiavelli's advice to play the animal well, being feared rather than loved, in favor of a good ruler who is "benevolent and virtuous . . . and will be loved as long as he is honest."[3] This good ruler must, above all, become the first servant of his state. The intention itself would determine a state's ultimate prosperity. Climbing further out on idealism's limb he made a noble case for honorable wars such as defense, precaution and legitimate interest.

"Interest" in this case exposed the nice point of Austrian deceit in trampling under Prussia's legitimate rights near Cologne, an absess still waiting to be lanced. Allies and treaties were necessities for protection, but might need to be broken for the same reason. Rationalizing that as long as allies were told ahead of time, convenient double speak, he claimed that such practice was acceptable, proving he already knew not only how to play the animal well, but how to rationalize his actions. He had grown up under a hard and unforgiving school and subsequently "cut his teeth" on playing the animal well.

In December 1739 twelve chapters of The Refutation went to Voltaire for editing. From his first years at Rheinsberg he had written back and forth as he worked on deconstructing Machiavelli's cynical arguments. Fritz's premise and style drew praise from the Philosophe in France along with a promise to write an introduction and see the project through to publication. The finished work appeared the following September. By then events had brought Fritz a world of new responsibilities into which he would fold his theses of moderation and servitude into the mash of fluctuating powers and duties of the throne of Prussia.

During the interim he was not idle. Elisabeth was put to work writing letters to her brothers in Wolfenbüttel asking for their contribution to the building up of Prussia's army with troops, money and participation as allies. Fritz was gambling on Prussia's efficient and sizeable standing force to right the wrongs of 1728 just as soon as power came into his hands, and Wolfenbüttel was a key starting point. While her brothers Karl and Ferdinand would have known she always looked out for Fritz's wishes first, her husband believed that family feeling toward their sister would persuade them to read her invitations and advice in

---

[3] Robert B. Asprey, Frederick the Great *The Magnificent Enigma*, (New York: Ticknor & Fields, 1986), 132.

more intimate terms. Accordingly, eight months before Fritz gained the crown, Elisabeth wrote to Karl.

> It is with much pleasure that I just received your obliging let-
> ter for which I note here my most perfect thanks, and read
> in it with the greatest joy in the world that your friendship
> for me continues to which I recommend myself again . . . . It
> would be a great joy for me if I could flatter myself to have
> the pleasure of seeing you. . . . the Prince advises you to as a
> good friend and asks you to give him this pleasure as well as
> me. I finish here as a good sister who loves you very tenderly
> . . . . I ask you to do me the justice of believing me with much
> tenderness and inviolable attachment . . .[4]

Given the formalities of the day and the fact that she was addressing an older brother and her father's heir, her excessive words can be taken as a dutiful sister's respect. It is equally clear, though, that she wanted to appear loyal to both home and husband. Three weeks later Karl sent her a birthday greeting in reply and opened an entering wedge for her to urge the Berlin visit once again.

> I just received your letter . . . and read in it with much plea-
> sure all of the good wishes that you give me . . . , and rec-
> ognize in those wishes new signs of your friendship for me
> . . . , you could soon give us signs of friendship by coming to
> Berlin. The Pr. R. who charges me to send you a thousand
> friendly greetings . . . asks you to give him the pleasure to
> come for something which is in the forefront, which is very
> important to us and which we wish that it succeeds, it is very
> important to you too and I advise you as a good friend to
> come, without which the thing could be pushed back, and
> our interests are involved. If it succeeds we will see it as a
> new sign of your friendship for us. You can well guess what it
> is if you remember the talk that we had when the king was in
> Brunswick and even the duchess will remember . . . . This will
> stay between us I hope and speak to you confidentially as to

---

[4] Elisabeth Christine letters Niedersächsisches Landesarchiv - Staatsarchiv Wolfenbüttel, 1 Alt 24. Nr. 288, Seite 36. 20 November 1739.

a brother whom I love with all my heart and of which I hope
to be persuaded that he will not betray me.[5]
Elisabeth was serving two masters and tense about it.
On the heels of her letters came further news that Karl's wife had
produced a "lovely princess" and mentions concern about the king's
health. A very human passage goes on:

> [I wish that] he [the king] will live a long time yet because
> for now I am happy with my state and we have equanimity
> and contentment although one wants more. I do not have
> this crazy ambition in my head to always want more, . . .
> and I find myself no happier being Princess Regent than I
> believe I would be were I Queen.[6]

Wisdom and self-knowledge in these words give the lie to history's
dismissal of Fritz's wife as insipid and stupid. Golden days in Rheinsberg had not blinded her to what lay ahead. Shortly Karl answered her,
promising to come. She was relieved, but still apprehensive. Fritz had
her in a sticky web as she replied

> . . . I saw in your letter that we will have the pleasure of
> seeing you . . . , and you will be able to make your case
> to the king . . . At the moment the thing in question goes
> very well. . . . I beg you not to speak of it to anyone except
> the Duchess Mother [their own mother, Antoinette Amalia]
> because no one should know that I am aware of the slight-
> est thing, without that everything would be taken care of
> because no one knows that I know that the Pr. R. spoke
> to me of it . . . . The pineapple that you sent gave us great
> pleasure and we admired it today and ate to your health.[7]

Again she assures Karl that, although the King had not gotten word of

---

[5] EC letters, Niedersächsisches Landesarchiv - Staatsarchive Wolfenbüttel, 1 Alt 24. Nr.
288, Seite 36.
[6] EC letters, Niedersächsisches Landesarchiv - Staatsarchive Wolfenbüttel, 1 Alt 24. Nr.
288, Seite 37. n.d.
[7] EC letters, Niedersächsisches Landesarchiv - Staatsarchive Wolfenbüttel, 1 Alt 24. Nr.
288, Seite 38, 26 November 1734. Pineapples being a delicacy and rarity in the north of
Germany at that time of year, it must have been a friendly echo from her sister-in-law
Philippine Charlotte, known to have been kind to her.

the visit to Berlin as yet,

> . . . he spoke yesterday of you the most graciously in the
> world and his mood grew increasingly good while speaking,
> also about the thing in question. He wants to see it finished
> soon, as for me I will not be displeased, especially before
> the other one learns of it and gets involved . . . . The Pr. R.
> asks me to give you many compliments from him, and to tell
> you that he will have a great joy to see you here again . . . .[8]

Within the month Karl and his wife arrived in Spandau at the king's
order, with several ladies and gentlemen of the court who "give themselves pleasure to see you, be persuaded that your presence will rejoice
us all and me in particular . . . ."

The king's last days of such graciousness were in any case nearly
used up. His regimen of binge and purge over the years had tortured a
body that at times spent days in agony, agitated by the medical advice
and care of the day which often aggravated and seldom soothed. Fritz
wrote Wilhelmina " . . . I foresee that we shall pass a sad winter."[9] Sad it
was. Gout, dropsy and shortness of breath dogged the days and sleep-
less nights.

Yet the king would not give in to a sickbed, calling his old friends together and for diversion, building wooden boxes and hammering away
at them while in bed. One day those gathered friends were caught in
a bind between two options. Fritz walked into the room unannounced
and reflex action brought them to their feet. It had never happened
before in Frederick William's presence, and his sense of his kingship
in spite of his weakness railed at their premature honor to a Crown
Prince.[10]

Toward the last of May Fritz became alarmed enough to travel to
Potsdam just in time to spend his father's last week of life with him.

---

[8] EC letters, Niedersächsisches Landesarchiv - Staatsarchive Wolfenbüttel, 1 Alt 24 Nr.
288, Seite 39, 1 December 1734. [" . . . the other one" refers to Fritz's sister Amelia,
the officious and headstrong future Abbess of Quedlinburg and Elisabeth's bête noire.]
[9] Asprey, 135.
[10] A not uncommon reaction of reigning sovereigns faced with their imminent demise.
Elizabeth I of England referred to her heir (and cousin, Mary Queen of Scot's son) James
I in the same vein near the end of her life.

Typical of Frederick William, their hours together were not wasted in sighs and tears, but used to bring Fritz up to date with affairs both inside and outside the country. Frederick William returned to Austria's betrayal as well as reservations about English and French designs. His bottom line was always - the army and the money. Keep both in your own hands: build up the army with new regiments, do not waste it in alliances where Prussia will have nothing to gain. Never go to war against Russia; an inevitable quagmire would result. Prussia's army was the best in Europe by any measure, equipment, training and discipline. As such it was the country's leverage against the bigger European states.

Even his funeral was discussed; predictably it was to be done on the cheap as much as possible. That last probably was a final flick of the finger at Frederick William's own profligate father, but it was a lesson to his spendthrift son. The crown to come would be serious business and Fritz had only lately begun to show that he was getting the message.

Bleedings and prayers went forward but this time the downward spiral would not be stopped. In the mid-afternoon of 31 May 1740 the king's body finally gave out, and he died trying to watch his face in a hand mirror in order to see what death looks like, in his case a hard fought battle lost at last. The mandatory postmortem proved his sheer iron will of mind over matter. Lungs, liver and gall bladder were diseased, decaying and past healing. Quarts of water were drained from the corpse before it was sent to the Potsdam's Garrison Church for burial.

Fritz wrote to Elisabeth that "God took the king this afternoon at half past three. You were in his thoughts." To Voltaire " . . . my destiny has changed."[11] Frederick William had sent a final farewell to Elisabeth shortly before the end came. It was a rare souvenir from the only full and loving heart in her seven years of marriage, the man who had ordered her life's fate, befriending her in spite of his wife's and family's distaste and disapproval.

> Madam, my daughter, I will always be indebted to you for the loving empathy which you carried for my dangerous situations of life . . . . If God does not answer your wishes, you will lose in me a father to whom you were above every-

[11] Asprey, 135.

thing very precious, and to whom I am connected with true friendship. Madam, your very good and faithful father.[12]

Evidence writ large and painful here illumines the downside of dynastic politics. The king had seen how able Elisabeth would be if his fractious son could only put forth the effort to understand her. But Fritz would never see it that way; his own station and brilliance deserved a wife with sharp and equally brilliant wit. Failing that, at the very least her devotion and loyalty should be absolute in light of the honor of marrying so high, but it should need no personal consideration.

He would give Elisabeth no quarter. She had failed to enlist her brothers for Fritz's cause, and he cast aside excuses about Wolfenbüttel's depleted finances. For him the details pro and con pointed to her family remaining in Austria's pocket. After all, her aunt was the wife of the emperor in Vienna, her dead father had been a general in the Austrian army, and her brothers were now backpedalling about helping Prussia. He had even offered to pay her debts if she could bring her family into his camp, to no avail. So be it; he turned his face from her.

Meanwhile mourning claimed his full attention as he sent the king's letter to his wife.

> Madam, the King was available this afternoon for three and one half hours, he thought about you and brought out from us [i.e. the royal "us"] honest tears of sympathy. You will not believe with how much strongness he died. You will, please come to Berlin, Wednesday or Thursday. ... we will live in our old house. As soon as you arrive, drive to Charlottenburg, you will immediately go to the Queen, to show your respect. And you will try to do more in this regard than usual. Then you may stay there as long as your presence is required, until I write to you. Try to see as few people as possible, or nobody. Tomorrow I shall put down the mourning of the ladies and to you will send my orders about that. Adieu, I hope to see you again in good health. I do not have time to write more, Adieu Féderic[13]

---

[12] Noack, 106.

[13] Noack, 106. Note the French version of his signature; his personal stamp of independence.

Before this letter got to Elisabeth over the sixty some miles (96 km.) from Potsdam to Rheinsberg, everyone had retired for the night. As Knobelsdorff appeared early the next Morning with the news that "the King is no more," Madame de Katsch prepared to greet Elisabeth as ". . . Majesty." Everyone at breakfast toasted the new reign and then, with an eighty horse train, the exodus from old life to new began. Fritz's orders also spelled out the procedure for the days ahead. Elisabeth read the signs along with the words and obeyed without question.

The hound of fortune was at her husband's heels. Great decisions needed to be made and grasping hands needed to be rapped right away. One of the first was the old king's military advisor and comrade in arms, Leopold of Dessau, asking that his position and authority be continued in the new reign. Fritz assured the old man that his position was safe, he "would not touch it, nor those of your sons," but authority was quite another thing. "I have become King; my intention is to carry out the functions of kingship and be the only one who has authority." Next, he called the expert on royal ceremonial from his grandfather's day and directed that all the black cloth needed be bought and the account sent to him, adding that no fee was to be taken from the draper. "I won't forgive that!"[14] From now on Fritz would make the decisions and pay the bills.

A single element remained of the great constraints of his youth: Elisabeth Christine. Held at arm's length after the funeral of her best friend, she yet was the nominal Queen of Prussia and as such guaranteed that Fritz would not, need not re-marry. Impatient embraces and the great marriage bed had become a dead issue.

---

[14] Gaxotte, Pierre Gaxotte, <u>Frederick the Great</u>. trans. R.A.Bell, (New Haven: Yale University Press, 1942), 174.

CHAPTER SEVEN

THE CARDBOARD QUEEN

Destiny claimed Elisabeth and Fritz on the day Frederick William died. The lyrical spirit of Remusberg dissolved overnight, submerged into the formal parade of their public roles. Elisabeth's part in Fritz's life, now that he was king, had been determined years before: she would go one way and he the other and "long live freedom." She had freed herself from the cocoon of awkward shyness in their four closely lived summers in Rheinsberg. Acceptance, even understanding, had seemed real enough. But it would never be; she would soon find that a forever separated life had begun. "The farce is over..." he told Fredersdorff, his man servant and only true confidant.[1]

They would live together at the Crown Prince's palace in Berlin for a time. She might hold Frederick William's last letter in her heart, but Fritz had no room in his schedule for such looking backward. His carefully crafted plans were already set to launch into the central European maelstrom. The vision of a new, outward bound Prussia focused his mind. Distractions, Elisabeth among them, were pushed aside and the lover of beauty and elegance in him began to wither his spirit away into xenophobia. Success at any cost, when it finally came, would be a lonely vindication.

Like a raptor eyeing its prey, he would force Prussia into the high stakes game of European power. Predictions that a dilettante was going to follow the Soldier King were dead wrong. Fritz was much more his father's son than that. His words from The Refutation about being the first servant of the state sounded mild, but they were snapped out by a hard-headed, furnace-tried despot.

His feverish haste laid on radical new forms of enlightened efficiency such as eliminating torture and the public flogging of unmarried mothers. Censorship of the press was ended. Freedom of religion was open to all as well as mandatory education for all children, with punishment for non-complying parents. An efficiently run state needed an informed and literate people. And it must be solvent. "Make a profit"

---

[1] Robert B. Asprey, Frederick The Great _The Magnificent Enigma_ (New York: Ticknor & Fields, 1986). 147.

was not served by his father's Lange Kerle (tall guys) regiment who were all pomp and exorbitant circumstance. They would have to go and be replaced with eight new battalions in the army. These were not the hedgy steps of a dilettante; he made them happen, putting himself at the head of each branch of government to bring it about. He would be his own chief minister, a ringmaster with the only whip. Free at last, but a clean sweep that forged its own bondage in the end.

Elisabeth became an adjunct in his staff, decorative and useful for essential ritual but put back into the closet until needed the next time. Her appearances continued but her essence as a partner in their marriage disappeared. Precious few letters came from Fritz, and no longer closed with eagerness to embrace her. He vanished as a mate, not by divorce nor exile nor replacing her with other women, but with crisp propriety. Numerous predictions about this had been given to Grumbkow and others before his engagement in 1732. Now, especially after she failed to rally support from her brothers for money and troops, the last chance for her to be a partner was gone.

On the morning when all this began she awakened a queen unaware, no longer a Crown Princess. Frau von Katsch greeted her as "Majesty" in the small bed she always used in Rheinsberg's large marriage chamber. Her little court gathered in the hall to swear their formal allegiance. Just as well that Fritz was not there, he would not bring himself to introduce her that formally when she joined him at Charlottenburg. He could rule without her, but his reign was going to need her.

First consideration was given to his mother. Sophia Dorothea must continue to call him "son," insisting it was much more meaningful between them than "Majesty." She was still a Queen, and her place in the pecking order unchanged, in his mind. However even she, and definitely his siblings, soon found that pecking order really meant nothing when expediency was crucial. Fritz never had any intention of allowing his mother a voice in great affairs. He personally set the details of formal Court mourning and his father's interment in Potsdam's Garrison Church. The old man had chosen that place himself to underscore his renown as the builder of a formidable army and efficient state, firmly ruling out showy parades. All the family was informed that Fritz now held them in thrall. He was the absolute court of last resort who intended his wishes to be obeyed without question. The heavy royal foot that had been so deeply imprinted on his own back was shifted now onto his siblings.

The royal pair moved into the Crown Prince's palace on Unter den Linden in Berlin for most of the early summer, in separate suites; there would be no pillow talk. When public display was obligatory, Elisabeth could appear with the family on the palace balcony, but only in the back row. All that mattered was that the king and queen be seen in some kind of public unity, and her height alone would ensure that. Near the end of July Fritz handed over the building to his younger brother, eighteen year old August William, at the same time declaring him the new "Prince of Prussia," the title reserved for the heir. No reason need be given. Tradition had always preserved royal marriages intact, even those loosely observed. Promoting his brother said more about distancing his wife than anything else.

The Berlin city palace became Fritz & Elisabeth's living quarters during winter and spring. She moved into a spacious third floor apartment that overlooked the River Spree, on the opposite side of the building from Fritz. Charlottenburg got a new wing at the same time, providing more space for family occasions such as the wedding two years later of August William to Elisabeth's sister Luise Amalie. Frederick William planned it before he died, to tie Wolfenbüttel's assets to Prussia's future. No more mistake about it, Elisabeth would be childless.

Fritz threw out the old tradition of inaugural tours to Brandenburg and East Prussia and coronations at Königsberg as a waste of time and thalers. A banquet was good enough and clearly Elisabeth would not be there. As a further sop, or a convenient riddance, Fritz had already given her Schönhausen, the summer home on the Panke river. Decidedly down-scale, it was built in the 1660's and bought by Frederick William's father in 1691. His son did not like the place and it was eventually used for office space. The old king had allowed Elisabeth to use it when Fritz was still in Ruppin, before they moved together into Rheinsberg.

By the summer of 1740 the deterioration of almost forty years was deplorable. But Fritz promised funds to renovate the house and reclaim the park, mercifully, since he had already run through what was left of Elisabeth's dowry income over the previous four years.   She loved the property, its modest size and country setting, and would live the next fifty-seven summers there with her small court and various members of her Wolfenbüttel family, but never with Fritz. It looked to be a kindly gift, but another step away from his personal life. Each now had separate leisure spaces alongside their obligatory winter and spring quarters in the Berlin city palace, where they were together but apart.

At the end of August Elisabeth looked over her new real estate with special house guests, the Princess of Anhalt-Zerbst and her eleven year old daughter, Sophia Augusta Fredericka. Sophia was a full-of-herself child, well known for her visit to Berlin as a four year old when she had taunted Frederick William with a cheeky remark about his ill fitting jacket. He laughed it away, but it probably caught a flicker of recognition between two downright, blunt personalities. Sophia was far from a sweet, thoughtful-of-others little girl, and five years after the Schönhausen visit she was climbing into the highest reaches of power as Prussia's preferred candidate for Tsarina, accompanied by her mother who was Fritz's paid informant at the Russian court in St. Petersburg.[2]

Fritz spent the last of summer into autumn laying the groundwork for getting Austria's harness off Prussia's neck. No longer should a lean, energetic state kowtow to an overfed, nearly bankrupt empire trading on its five centuries old roots. He had the best trained army in Europe, 83,000 strong, and reasoned that other states were already debating their own chances to pluck off some fruit from Austria's orchard. Silesia, on the northeastern flank of Austrian territory with mineral wealth in lead, zinc, iron and coal was worth going after right away.

Besides being the best territory within his reach, Fritz saw an untried twenty-three year old female ready to edge herself onto the Austrian throne, limply supported by a near empty treasury and a council of advisors captive to their own pessimism. The fact that she was his wife's first cousin mattered not at all. This was business. Speed and secrecy versus a too little, too late response from the Austrians might just net this catch . Scornfully, he described the fifty-five year old Emperor in Vienna accurately, and cynically, as

> the old ghost of an idol which once had power and was mighty, but which is of no account today. He used to be a strong man but the French and the Turks have given him the pox and nowadays he is feeble."[3]

---

[2] The Wolfenbüttel-Romanov connection is described in a later page in this chapter.
[3] Pierre Gaxotte, Frederick the Great (New Haven: Yale University Press, 1942), 193.

On 20 October the old ghost abruptly died in Vienna. He had suffered a "chill" while out hunting and then added to his misery by eating a plate of mushrooms which had given him indigestion; probably modern medicine would point to symptoms of a heart attack.[4] In the eighteenth century, however, no one expected a fifty-five year old to die from what was a regular result of the royal table. Tenacious to the end, Charles VI could not believe the inevitable and ordered that his doctor kill himself after performing a postmortem examination of the imperial corpse, so that the cause of death could be explained when they both reached paradise.

The staggering news reached Rheinsberg on the 26th when Fritz was sick in bed and he wrote to Voltaire

> This death destroys all my peaceable thoughts [!] and I think for the next month it will be more a matter of powder, soldiers and trenches . . . .[5]

broadly hinting he meant the end of the imperial status quo. Right away he roused body and strength to bring about a new order in the Germanies, with Prussia leading the way. Only two days later, Fritz was conferring with advisors at Rheinsberg about exactly how they would make the most of this opportunity.

Voltaire was expected to arrive shortly and Fritz needed a hostess. It would be the last time he and his wife were to receive a guest together in their own house and the last time Elisabeth was there. The Frenchman never had appealed to her. His freewheeling ideas about religion upset her own too sharply. Happily, Voltaire did not arrive until early November when Elisabeth was gone. She wrote to her brother Karl that Voltaire's visit would perk up her husband but adding cryptically that ". . . he seems to be what he is . . . ."[6]

Voltaire's journey tried him to the boiling point with bad roads and

---

[4] "Chill" was a recurrent cause of royal deaths; Philip the Handsome of Spain drank ice water following a brisk tennis match, his doctors claimed in 1506, and removed himself from Spain's line of succession.

[5] Ludwig Reiners, <u>Frederick the Great a Biography</u>, (New York: G.P. Putnam's Sons, 1960), 92.

[6] Elisabeth Christine letters. Niedersächsisches Landesarchiv - Staatsarchiv Wolfenbüttel, 1 Alt 24. Nr. 288. Seite 00158.

worse weather, finally arriving in the village to be challenged at the entrance gate. It was not their smoothest reunion. Fritz had already begun tempering his hero worship and his cup of irritation ran over when the Philosophe presented a bill for his expenses in getting Antimachiavel published and marketed as well as the cost of traveling to Prussia. Always looking to pay from someone else's purse, Fritz exploded.

> . . . [The] miser will drink the very dregs of his insatiable desire to get rich . . . [a] visit of a week will cost me five hundred livres per diem. . . . fine price to pay for a madman; never did a jester get such a good wage.[7]

Adding insult to injury Voltaire put down Fritz's proposed invasion of Austria, but by now his advice carried no weight. Fritz was determined to show the world his mettle while gaining a premium new province.

Words in the Antimachiavel about recognizing "legitimate interest" as a case for defensive war came in handy now. He had claimed in print that an enemy could legitimately be put on notice that armed conflict was contemplated with, in this instance, the self-serving excuse that offering protection to his wife's cousin against threats from nearly every power wanting to pare away at the Pragmatic Sanction was really a form of family solidarity. All it would cost was ceding Silesia to Prussia in exchange for Fritz's army coming to Maria Theresia's "rescue." On 20 December this cynical proposal was handed to Vienna. A reply would be immaterial. By the time it arrived Frederick and his army were well across the Silesian border. Secrecy and stealth were everything. Fritz and Elisabeth danced at a masked ball in Berlin on the ninth of January and the invasion began three days later.

Comparison is irresistible between the two granddaughters of Brunswick-Wolfenbüttel: Elisabeth Christine in Berlin and Maria Theresia in Vienna. The former married to an iron personality and herself powerless, the latter a latent but soon activated iron will married to an also-ran. Despite some early pussyfooting and even fleeing the battlefield a time or two, Fritz gained his nerve as well as his balance, drove his troops ahead to victory and began his crusade for Prussia's future. Silesia was lost to Austria from 1741 on when peace was finally signed

---

[7] Gaxotte, 187.

at the Treaty of Berlin in 1742. Along with a no-contest victory, considering the debilitated state of the empire, Fritz gained a bitter, grudge-bearing enemy in Maria Theresia. His cocky suggestion of marrying her years before was turned on its head. Austria was put in her place, definitely below Prussia. Maria Theresia was now the Apostolic Hag to him, and Fritz the Robber of Silesia to her.

Three antagonists, Austria, Prussia and Russia, would pick at their sores from the beginning to nearly the end of the eighteenth century. Ironically, the tenuous adhesive patching their edges together was the small, ambitious duchy of Brunswick-Wolfenbüttel and the marriages arranged with them by Habsburg, Hohenzollern and Romanov in the first chapter of this book. Moving onward into the century, the Russian Tsar Peter the Great's irregular private life (1672-1725) both before and after his son's death contrived to get a confused bag of heirs and a mistress/wife, Catherine I with whom he had fathered two daughters, Anne and Catherine who added their own claims to succeed him.

When Peter died his former mistress and legitimized tsarina grabbed the crown herself. She did not survive long; after her death primogeniture regained its bearings when the underage orphaned son of Alexis and Charlotte Christine of Brunswick-Wolfenbüttel succeeded as Tsar Peter II. Raised by regents whose main responsibility seems to have been their own leverage, they betrothed him to one of their own daughters. He was crowned, aged 13, in 1728 and wed, supposedly mature, two years later on the same day he died of smallpox. Appallingly, if anecdotal evidence can be credited, she was slipped into his bed during that fateful day in hopes he might have the stamina to impregnate her before he died. It was not successful.

After such a fiasco, the Romanovs went through a decade of unpopular feminine rule that ended with the death of Peter's elder daughter, the childless empress Anne, two months after the birth of a male successor, the great-nephew of Peter the Great and future Tsar Ivan VI. This baby was born in St. Petersburg very close to the same day that Elisabeth and her guests, the future Catherine the Great and her mother were arriving at Schönhausen in August of 1740. Before leaving Berlin Elisabeth had written to her younger brother Anton Ulrich, married to Anna Leopoldovna, Peter the Great's niece, the previous year in St. Petersburg and the father of this child, about the "happy delivery" of his son, with congratulations on the baby's "ascendancy of [sic] the throne ... all will come out for your good and advantages."[8]

Advantages looked to begin right away when Anna Leopoldovna, the baby's mother, was appointed Regent for her two week old son, but good advantage lasted a mere four months. A palace coup d'etat led by Peter the Great's last living offspring, forty-one year old Elisabeth (Anna's aunt) swept the plans aside. Childless, but ready to hand with a two year old nephew who would be made her heir, the power, the steely will and the brass ring were all hers.

Anna Leopoldovna, Anton Ulrich and their son Ivan VI, were taken under guard to prison in Riga, Latvia. Not long afterwards, worry about German or other relatives' support for their return to Russia sealed their fate, and they were sent even further away to Kholmogory, 470 miles (750 km.) north of St. Petersburg near the waters of the White Sea. Ivan was held apart from his parents until he was finally murdered in 1764 on the express orders of the girl, now grown, who had been Prussia's candidate in 1744 as a wife for the Empress Elisabeth's heir. No longer Sophia Augusta Fredericka of Anhalt-Zerbst, she was recast as Catherine Alexeyevna at her baptism into the Russian Orthodox faith and eventually became the great Catherine II, the brazen adolescent who had visited Schönhausen with Elisabeth Christine in 1740.

---

[8] EC letters, Niedersächsisches Archiv - Staatsarchiv Wolfenbüttel, 1 Alt 22. Nr. 771, Seite 32-33.

The ducal palace in Wolfenbüttel, south of Braunschweig. Elisabeth Christine's childhood home, the Kleines Schloss or small palace, is across the moat on the left. Author photo.

Schloss Rheinsberg in the lake country north of Berlin is the only home Elisabeth and Fritz shared together. Author photo.

Young Fritz, shortly after becoming king. Prussian Foundation for Castles and Gardens, Berlin-Brandenburg. Photo by Roland Handrick.

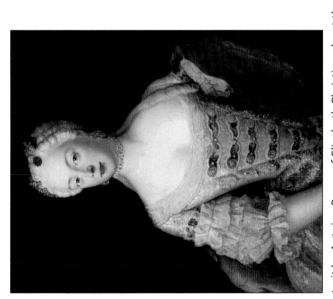

A portrait by Antoine Pesne of Elisabeth Christine about the time of her marriage to Fritz in 1733 at Salzdahlum near Wolfenbüttel. Archives of Prussian Foundation for Castles and Gardens, Berlin-Brandenburg. Photo by Roland Handrick.

Fritz, now called Frederick the Great after fighting his wars. Prussian Foundation for Castles and Gardens, Berlin-Brandenburg. Photo by Jörg P. Anders.

Queen Elisabeth Christine in old age after Fritz's death. Prussian Foundation for Castles and Gardens, Berlin-Brandenburg. Photo by Frédéric Reclam.

Schönhausen, Elisabeth's summer home in Pankow, a northeastern suburb of Berlin. It has been beautifully restored recently. Author photo.

Sans Souci, Frederick the Great's "pleasure palace" in Potsdam. The flat tombstones in the foreground are for his dogs. Fritz's tomb (inset) is to the right of his dogs. Author photo.

CHAPTER EIGHT

WEDDED WAR WIDOWS

"Schönhausen never seemed to be more beautiful to me than now . . . ."[1] A soft summer morning flows through Elisabeth's words in 1745. Life was becalmed after two years of war, siege and blunder had ended with a grudging peace in 1742. Silesia was gathered into Prussia. At times Fritz had managed to be a fleeting presence in Berlin between battles, appearing with Elisabeth at court events, even the opera. Now that the war was over that propagandizing had done its work. Austria's defenses were exposed as the impaired and incompetent force they had become, and Prussia made good on Frederick William's vow that Fritz would avenge the Habsburgs' double dealing of the past. That completed, Fritz could turn his back on the social rituals of Berlin for a time and hand over royal appearances to Elisabeth.

He used the respite to focus on building a summer retreat of his own in Potsdam, twenty miles (32 km.) southwest of the capital. It became the small gem of Sans Souci,[2] located on a knoll looking over a vineyard and the nearest he would ever come to recapturing the spirit of Rheinsberg. He wanted it to be intimate and restful, following his own taste and eventually becoming known as Frederician Rococo. The Rheinsberg coterie were fewer in number, Knobelsdorff and Jordan dying within months of each other in 1745, but new friends appeared to fill the void. He opened the palace with a grand soirée in May of 1747.

Elisabeth of course was not invited. In fact, she knew by then it was best not to hope for a visit there at any time. Schönhausen had come with a price tag - complete detachment from his private life. Her presence, and her value, was restricted to proper ceremonial, which meant her days would be spent on a beaten path between formality and protocol in Berlin two-thirds of the year, and at Schönhausen as long as summer allowed.

The illusion of "Remusberg" dissolved in 1741 as Fritz went away to war; its gracious dinners and lyrical evenings with sophisticated con-

---

[1] Paul Noack, <u>Elisabeth Christine und Friedrich der Grosse Ein Frauenleben in Preussen</u> (Stuttgart: Klett-Cotta, 2001) 119.
[2] "without care"

versation wisped into memory. Elisabeth's attendants were rearranged: Katsch was ordered to give way to Charlotte von Kannenberg, who was traded up to Katsch's post as Court Mistress. Abrupt demotion after seven years of service was hard to swallow and Katsch wrote to Fritz lamenting the change, a mark "of disgrace of which I feel the deepest despair."[3] Fritz breezily responded that his decision was completely neutral, Katsch was ". . . not from the country,"[4] adding that none of the courts of Europe had foreigners in such a position - a shaky argument since Katsch's husband had been a Justice Minister in Berlin until his death in 1729. She had no leverage for debate with him but gamely raised the point of being pushed down into sixth place in the queen's retinue.

Her three years of guiding a timid, abandoned bride in Berlin, expected to overcome the roadblocks of Fritz's family and Berlin society itself, followed by another three and a half years at Rheinsberg where Elisabeth grew to be a social partner in his life ought not end so offhandedly. He was not denying Katsch's value, Fritz quickly pointed out. He would "never stop giving . . . credit for her worthy qualities." She should not brood about rank; he appreciated her and would look for ways to convince her, closing with "your affectionate King Frederick."[5] Rank, in other words, was his concern.

A new dogma had captured Fritz: the Enlightenment and its faith in rationalism that had been exciting the minds, and frightening the crowns, since the mid-1600's. Fritz had spent long hours in study at Rheinsberg and before, soaking up his new "religion" like healing balm poured over a long tried spirit, validating his determination to bring on a new model of Prussian government and society. He had gone along with accepting a second string wife and a dull marriage, and their first five years together chained to shopworn convention. Katsch's aggravating deep curtseys when Remusberg evenings skirted over the line of "propriety" had galled him long enough. Now with Elisabeth tucked away at Schönhausen and himself off in Potsdam, far fewer holds were

---

[3] Elisabeth Christine Letters, Niedersächsisches Landesarchiv - Staatsarchiv Wolfenbüttel, 1 Alt 24 Nr. 288, Seite 0143.
[4] EC Letters, N.L. - S.W., 1 Alt 24 Nr. 288, 0144.
[5] EC Letters, N.L. - S.W., 1 Alt 24 Nr. 288, 0143.

barred. Six years later he was still chewing over the memories, telling August William who wanted to include Elisabeth on an outing: "If my prudish sourpuss takes part she will, I fear, ruin the whole thing."[6]

In 1742 Fritz appointed Countess Sophie Caroline de Camas as Court Mistress for Elisabeth. Her husband, Paul Henry Tilio de Camas had recently died while on a mission to the French court at Versailles. Kannenberg's brief promotion had probably been a stopgap; Sophie Camas must have been in Fritz's plans all the time. The Camas' were tried and true friends from the old days when he lived at home. His "Bon maman," as he always addressed her in letters, was created a countess to make her acceptable in the circle of his wife's ladies. The new countess knew the *manières*[7] as well as the sharp intelligence that drove him, but at the same time realized Elisabeth's lot. Now there would be a balanced voice between them, one they both could trust, and Camas had the strength of character to give each his due and serve them well. Over the next twenty-four years she became their sage counselor. Fritz, well known as a sparing gift giver, favored Camas with a pricey set of Meissen china, a be-jeweled snuff box, and a diamond ring over the years. She herself was an even greater gift to mistress and master.

Only some half dozen letters arrived from Sans Souci during Elisabeth's first two years at Schönhausen. They closed with "complete respect," the baseline of his feelings for her. He would no longer write of love between them. Respect, impersonal and distant, was her due and he relied on that. The marriage bed left behind in Rheinsberg, sexual feelings for Fritz were only acceptable now with a lower caste, possibly the dancer Barberina Campanella at Sans Souci as rumors later hinted, or young men of his personal entourage. The youthful Dresden escapade had left a residue, physical and emotional. As he summed up for Voltaire, living for the self alone was better than living for others.[8]

Cynical about everyone and everything, a mindset that fitted his enlightened beliefs, easily led to a suspicion of loyalty any and everywhere which never left his mind. Elisabeth was regularly baited about

---

[6] Robert B. Asprey, <u>Frederick The Great *The Magnificent Enigma*</u> (New York: Ticknor & Fields, 1986), 389.
[7] Pretended indifference.
[8] Noack, 120.

her brothers: Karl in cahoots with the English, Ferdinand the same with Austria, even far away Anton Ulrich with Russia. Near the end of April 1742 she was able to show her own loyalty, telling Fritz she had heard that Vienna planned to kill him. Putting fears into words must have cost her, and for once he answered with grace.

> Madam, one has to love you, if one knows you, and the goodness of your heart is deserving, such that one recognizes that. I am endlessly obliged to you for the effort which you put into it, to prove the news, which was brought to you.[9]

Three weeks before this exchange, suspicion had gotten the best of him and Elisabeth wrote Karl about a letter in which Fritz pointed a finger at her family's designs.

> The King believes that you are not his friend. He writes a letter to me today in which he does nothing else but insult my family and says that he will avenge himself in a terrible way for everything that my family has done to him.[10]

In that pre-digital age such an inflammatory letter would burn the receiver for days or weeks before another arrived to resolve the anger and suspicion. "Living for self alone" was surely at work in it. Elisabeth asked Karl to convince their mother not to write to Vienna so much, a tacit acknowledgement of tampering with the mails.

The year 1742 was a watershed for Fritz. Before that he was honing his craft and after it he drove resolutely straight ahead, never giving in. The next step would be a guarantee against losing Silesia: alliance with Saxony and help from France, for which Camas's husband had been negotiating before his untimely death. In these crucial years Fritz squeezed every asset he had, which included badgering his wife and her family. The centuries old lineup of allies and rivals across the continent was fraying at the edges and ready to be turned on its head by a lean, mean and well-funded strong arm.

Allies were personal insurance and began at home. In January of 1742, six months before peace over Silesia was signed, Fritz marched his brother August William, his heir as Prince of Prussia, to the al-

[9] Noack, 121.
[10] Noack, 122.

tar and marriage to Luise Amalia of Brunswick Wolfenbüttel, Elisabeth's younger, and favorite, sister. The same purpose that wed Fritz to Elisabeth nine years earlier now brought about William's marriage to another Wolfenbüttel. Arbitrarily, Elisabeth was barred from the ceremony. ". . . the King wished that I remain here (in her apartment in the Berlin palace). I have to abide by this."[11] But she made up for it by appearing at the wedding gala afterward in a bejeweled green velvet robe and a blazing emerald tiara on her head.

Though William obeyed Fritz's orders at the altar, his roving eye never stopped hunting. Fritz had hammered him down to accept the somber fact that marriage was business, not to be confused with besottedness, love or even fidelity. The succession, as well as hanging onto allies, was at stake. William had his own role in Hohenzollern destiny and Brunswick must stay in its pocket and purse. Within two years both marriage and begetting of heir and "spare" were fulfilled. The elder son, and first of four more Frederick Williams in future generations, eventually succeeded as Frederick William II in 1786, but fatherhood did not change William; "The Prince of Prussia likes every woman better than his wife."[12]

Fritz's next younger brother, Henry, was given Rheinsberg in 1744 when he was eighteen, and over his lifetime he lavished as much care on it as Fritz had. Driving ambition joined with love of music and art and a preference for male companionship set him apart from William and Ferdinand, the youngest boy. Henry finally married at twenty-six to Princess Wilhelmine of Hesse-Cassel, his own age, a match forced upon him. There were never any children and after 1770 she spent her summers with the "war widows" living at Schönhausen.

Separation between Elisabeth and Fritz gradually became the accepted norm in Prussian society. From the game-changing moment of the Emperor's death in Vienna through the next twenty-three years, Fritz gambled his army and war chest on Prussia's growing power. Living in saddle and army camp, and hanging ceremonial duty in Berlin on Elisabeth's shoulders, he chased the glory to be had on the fields of Mars.

Any time away from fighting was spent on enriching his architectur-

---

[11] Noack, 124.
[12] Asprey, 391.

al magnum opus, the diminutive jewel of Sans Souci. Departed friends of Rheinsberg were replaced by talkers and bon mots invited into the presence but not always into the heart. Wit and cleverness were everything and Voltaire, forgiven after his disastrous visit to Rheinsberg in 1740, was again welcomed with open arms, at least in the beginning. He had not changed his taking ways, unfortunately, in spite of Elisabeth's entertaining him beforehand in Berlin. Not destined to last, soon enough togetherness at Sans Souci had run its course and within two years it was finished for good. Fritz's biographer Pierre Gaxotte observed, "Potsdam was too small to house two kings."[13]

Occasionally women were bidden to Sans Souci, his sisters and mother and the rest of his family, but never his wife. Frau Camas, Kannenberg and other members of the Schönhausen court dined there, ". . . received with excellent attention and amiability,"[14] Elisabeth wrote in 1746. They also celebrated New Year's eve with Fritz several years running. But Elisabeth's place was elsewhere greeting visiting royals, nobles and foreign ambassadors. Family occasions were pointedly denied her as in July of 1746 when they all gathered at Oranienburg, William's country home north of Berlin. William apologized to Elisabeth but told her that he did not dare go against orders, he had no starch for a fight he would certainly lose. It was very hard, she wrote to her brother Ferdinand.

> My sister is also going. I shall keep the palace in the meanwhile, and be my nephew's governess. I am very glad that my sister is going; it will be at least a pleasure to her, and it is as it ought to be. I am very glad that there is nobody but myself forsaken and obliged to put up with mortifications; if my sister were treated in the same way, it would be a double vexation for me. The Prince of Prussia asked me the other day whether it would be agreeable to me if he were to leave my sister here to keep me company. I replied that though I was always very happy to see my sister, [he] might be well assured that if he took her with him to Oranien-

---

[13] Pierre Gaxotte, <u>Frederick the Great</u> trans. R. A. Bell (New Haven: Yale University Press, 1942), 257.
[14] Noack, 133.

burg, it would give me much greater pleasure . . . . There-
upon he wanted to speak about myself; but I replied . . . I
was accustomed to it, but . . . it would increase my distress
if . . . my sister was . . . put on the same footing as myself.[15]

Henry had been warned off too, and Elisabeth told him to go ahead
with inviting Luise to Rheinsberg and "not let her be treated like me."
By now, Fritz's siblings had learned who was boss. It was easier for ev-
erybody just to get along by going along with the drill at Potsdam.

All this rejection began to take its toll on Elisabeth, writing in 1747:

For myself, I do not longer wish anything more than to
win the great ticket at the Frankfurt lottery to pay with it
my debts. After that I can peacefully expect death, if God
deems it good, to take me from this world, in which I have
nothing to do any more . . . .[16]

Pining for Fritz's company when a chance visit brought him to Schönhausen:

I will keep this totally in secret, so that the family does not
get [to know of it] because then one would try at once to
prevent this, because all of them are jealous of the smallest
grace which he shows to me.[17]

Inevitably the underlying lament surfaces: "why has everything become so different, why did I have to lose all the former goodness and
grace . . . ."[18]

Camas's influence was showing by the end of the decade.

The King wishes to be alone in the family circle . . . . If I follow the advice of the Camas I will not go to Berlin at all. But
I believe it would be better if I would do this, because otherwise it looks like . . . I would play the hurt one, or the ex-

---

[15] Andrew Hamilton, <u>Rheinsberg: Memorials of Frederick the Great and Prince Henry of Prussia in two volumes 1 & 2</u> (London: J. Murray, 1880) II, 23-4.
[16] Noack, 142. Letter to her brother Ferdinand.
[17] Noack, 142. Also to Ferdinand. The "one" referred to was Princess Amelia, Fritz's youngest sister and reportedly an "enfant terrible" during her childhood; now bound to spinsterhood and taking care of her aging mother. Fritz had had her highly unsuitable marriage in 1743 quickly annulled. She ended her days as the Abbess of Quedllinburg.
[18] Noack, 143. Again to Ferdinand.

clusive one or the ridiculous one . . . . Only God knows, that I think of nothing else, night and day than to prevent, what could happen to him. It is very difficult for me, to know him in Berlin, without being allowed to see him.[19]

It goes on, debating the possible result if she did see him, but in the end she gives it up and stays home. Camas knew that Fritz was not handling his family with any more consideration than he handled Elisabeth. She could gain nothing by shoving herself into his presence; annoying his family or avoiding them were equally immaterial. Following orders was her best bet as Camas wisely advised. The great questions of the day had overtaken her husband's mind and his plans had priority over everything and everyone else.

At the same time, serious money problems were piling up on Elisabeth's ledger. They had been growing since Rheinsberg days when Fritz's spendy ways often dipped into her resources. Over the years since she had countersigned loan requests for him and listened to his promises of financial help. Now accounts were coming in that could not be met with either good intentions or royal promises. The letter she wrote to Karl on 7 November 1752 is one case.

> Much obliged for your dear letter and wish you much health and happiness during your trip, pardon me for including a letter here, you will see by the content what it is about, this is the third I have received of this type. I ask you dear brother to advise me what I should reply, and if it is possible be so kind as to take care of it for me, I will be infinitely obliged, I find myself terribly uncomfortable with this, you know dear brother my situation but one cannot say it openly to strangers, who think one swims in gold.[20]

She enclosed the letter in question from a Henriette P. D. Waldeck on 30 October 1752:

> Your Majesty, if I were not persuaded of the very Royal feelings that you possess Mme. I would not have taken the liberty in my previous letter, to put in front of her eyes the

---

[19] Noack, 144. To Ferdinand.
[20] EC letters, N. L. - S.W., 1 Alt 24, 291.

state in which I find myself, and to beg her very humbly, to rescue me, with two thousand écus, I do not doubt at all, that my letters have been delivered to YM, but I imagine Mme., that you have reasons, that keep YM's generous heart from following its desires, of grace I would therefore take the liberty of making a proposition, HH the Duke brother of YM who knows my state, and has already given me tokens of his respect, in many occasions, would take it upon himself to pay the two thousand écus, so that it will remain unknown to everyone, and YM will be able to reimburse M. the Duke surely, take pity YM think about this proposal, and if it is possible to relieve a person whose heart is respectfully attached to You great and worthy Queen, hope sustains me, God knows my thoughts, and how much . . . .[21]

Into the bargain, the king's siblings were proving almost as difficult to handle as Fritz had been himself. Nearly half a generation separated him from his younger brothers William, Henry and Ferdinand, with four sisters in between. Brotherly feeling was strong among them but Fritz stood apart and above now that he was head of the family. Decisions were his to make and theirs to follow. William, his heir, had married as ordered. Eighteen year old Henry was living at Rheinsberg, also as ordered, and fourteen year old Ferdinand could wait a year or two for his marching orders. The inescapable Army was bred into each of their futures regardless of fitness or desire. All three had been in uniform and regiment from birth.

Their brides did little better than Elisabeth, but in William's case infidelities were lesser ills than his catastrophic mistakes. Given a command in 1756 at the outset of the Seven Years War,[22] he watched Prussia's early victories being squashed by Austria which went on to officially expel Prussia from the Holy Roman Empire. Fortunes were slipping for Prussia. By early June of 1757 William's ever uncertain nerve failed him when he was given the vital task of protecting food and armament

[21] EC Letters, N.L. - S.W., 1 Alt 24, 291.
[22] The Seven Years War, 1756-1763, was the conflict between Austria, France, Russia, Britain and Prussia over predominance in Europe and between Britain and France in North America.

supplies for 40,000 troops at Zittau, on the Saxon border. He dithered between frantic calls for Fritz's orders and packing his bags for retreat. In the end, the latter won out and he was pulled from his post by an infuriated brother.

> Command a harem, fine, but as long as I live you will have no detachment greater than ten men. When I am dead, you may commit as much folly as you like; it'll be on your head, but as long as I live you will do nothing more to damage the state. That is all I have to say to you. Let your best officers clean up the shambles you have made . . . . What I say is hard but true.[23]

All accounts of this fiasco leave the clear impression that William caved in under pressure, unable to make any decisive move on his own. More to the point, Fritz's back was against the wall and his heir had failed him utterly; his gamble to stop the Austrians in their tracks was lost. Fritz had always treated William as a useful appendage, but arrogant expectations and pre-emptive commands had rashly ignored the weaker mettle he had placed in command. There is a telling parallel here with Frederick William's taunting words after forcing an adolescent Fritz to kiss his boots.

Anger had mixed with regret for both brothers by the time that Sophia Dorothea died two weeks later. Losing a mother he sincerely loved and counted on, however, did not call up Fritz's forgiveness for a brother who had let him down so completely. "He deserves to have his head chopped off . . . ."[24] Fritz told his generals. They were probably relieved when Fritz broke off contact with William. "Do what you want; I shall not concern myself any more with your circumstances."[25] Six months later William was dead, some said of a broken heart. Fritz's attitude had only hardened. "It is a theme which afflicts me greatly, but I simply don't have time to cry."[26] Twentieth century research more closely describes a cerebral hemorrhage due to a brain tumor as the cause of William's death.

---

[23] Giles McDonogh, <u>Frederick The Great *A Life in Deed and Letters*</u> (London, Phoenix Press, 1999), 257.

[24] McDonogh, 257.

[25] McDonogh, 258.

[26] McDonogh, 259.

Luise spent her summers after that with Elisabeth at Schönhausen. She had done her duty and supplied two children: a son and acknowledged heir, and a daughter who would produce another heir, to the kingdom of the Netherlands. Later Henry's discarded Wilhelmina of Hesse-Cassel would arrive. Conversation and common cause between the three of them at Schönhausen must have been intense, but in the end had no effect. The offspring of Frederick William and Sophia Dorothea were a fraternity unto themselves. At least it proved to Elisabeth that the cold and careless treatment she received was not exceptional. Compassion was a limited commodity which rarely ever reached outside that blood royal circle and marriages generated no personal feelings. The royal war widows, rejected discards cut off from husbands at the front, all knew it, but in Elisabeth's case she had had the misfortune to fall in love, and bitterness began to invade her spirit.

Fritz put his losses, personal and political, into the back of his mind after the debacle at Zittau. Time was ripe to follow up on his gains. Prussia had moved into British orbit in January 1756 with a neutrality agreement not to allow France, or anyone else, to cross German lands and attack Hannover, Britain's old toehold on the continent. Austria, Britain's former ally, had ratted out to join France and Fritz feared having to defend his borders on the west as well as on the east. Saxony to the south was sizing up its chances in Upper Silesia and Moravia. There would be none of that; Fritz slid into the driver's seat, invaded and defeated Saxony in 1756 and followed up with victory against the Austrians in Bohemia by the end of 1757, despite the Russian Tsarina Elisabeth sending troops to Austria's aid.

His new arrangements became the blasting cap for a diplomatic revolution, upsetting the old balance of power in Europe. Sagas of the Seven Years War overflow with the strategic brilliance of Fritz and his army. Defeats and victories kept him on the move, in appalling conditions. His father's tomb in Potsdam must have rumbled when Prussia was thrown out of the Empire, but Fritz was creating a new Europe and his personal debilities and discomforts were stoically accepted. Austria was the past, he and Prussia would be the future.

His wife lived through those days doing her best to support his cause and she began to find her own place to stand in a fervent religious belief. She would need that support for the rest of her life. For

safety's sake in mid-October 1757, Elisabeth and her court were ordered to leave the Berlin palace for the fortress at Spandau, eight and
a half miles (14 km.) to the west. They were not there long but sent
farther out of harm's way to Magdeburg, ninety miles (145 km.) to the
southwest. Following the rout at Zittau the Austrians were making for
Berlin. If the Prussian government could be taken prisoner and more
significantly its treasury looted, the game would be up there and then.

Five days after leaving Spandau the queen and her attendants entered the gates of Magdeburg, to the general rejoicing of the popula-
tion who welcomed them with food and drink. Elisabeth returned their
greeting with a banquet that evening at the recently built fortress and
for the next two months she and her retinue were safe. On her way
between Spandau and Magdeburg she and her large train had passed
through Potsdam, reportedly the only time she was ever in the town.
It was pointed out, by those who dared, that it had taken an Austrian
army to get her through the town gates since her husband had never
allowed it. Visiting Wolfenbüttel was off limits, in spite of the fact that it
was only sixty miles (96 km.) from Magdeburg. The leash was still short.

By the beginning of 1758, with the Prussian army gaining several
victories, Elisabeth could return to Berlin and her usual summer retreat
of Schönhausen. In May Fritz wrote a letter to Henri de Catt, a new
member of his personal staff, that contained the most even and mature
view of his marriage.

> One is dependent of one another and must be . . . con-
> siderate of one another. One learns to be silent about
> critique and blame. Confidence among ourselves creates
> trust. Even if I, unfortunately, could not feel passion for the
> Queen, so was our togetherness in Rheinsberg yet almost
> tender. Why is it my fault . . . that the war did not leave me
> with either time or choice to continue this unity? As soon
> as I will be in Potsdam, I will look for her. She is totally as-
> sured of my honoring her.[27]

It had been twenty-five years in coming; the angry newlywed overlaid
by a semi-apologist husband. Elisabeth had proved herself obedient,

---

[27] Noack, 186.

honorable and loyal along with still tender feelings for him. He knew he could count on her. She responded as expected the following month when news came of William's death at Oranienburg and Elisabeth had to break the news to her sister. In spite of William's weaknesses it was a sad time and Elisabeth wrote a letter to Fritz asking for his leave to allow Antoinette Amalia to visit her daughters at Schönhausen. It had to be carefully crafted to avoid Fritz's suspicions about any Wolfenbüttel plotting.

> I promise ... not the slightest intrigue will take place . . . . I will not spend more than is necessary . . . . I will do nothing to call forth your displeasure.[28]

Fritz knew more than enough to realize his sister-in-law Luise, the mother of his new heir, needed a kind hand. Probably he acknowledged the same was also deserved by his wife, so Antoinette Amalia was permitted to make the visit.

The fighting wore on for another two years. In the late summer of 1759 Fritz's army suffered a major defeat that sent his wife and her supporters flying back to Magdeburg for another three years in the governor's house. Fortunately she carried Schönhausen's valuables with her for safekeeping, but once there she kept to a regular personal routine, showing herself on walks along the Elbe river, as an encouragement to the citizens. Her escape was none too soon. The Russian army entered Berlin in early October and after a matter of days arrived at Schönhausen, hell bent to sack the palace and carry off its treasure. All that had been left in place to block "these cruel monsters without any inner religion," were her steward and his wife.

> On the seventh of October [1760] came ten Cossacks to the . . . castle, demand[ing] money and especially the silver dishes of her majesty. They received one hundred thaler and were told there were no silver dishes because her majesty always eats from porcelain. [The next] morning came an officer and eight hussars who demanded . . . the royal silver. They . . . tore down all the wallpaper, drapes, chairs,

---

[28] Catherine E. Hurst, <u>Elizabeth Christine, Wife of Frederick the Great, from German and Other Sources</u> (New York: Phillips & Hunt, Cincinnati: Walden & Stowe, 1880), 143-4.

couches and even her majesty's bed, forced open all closets and cupboards and took everything they liked. . . . then went to the house of the Steward . . . took him and his wife into the living room, stripped them both naked, beat him with sticks and whips . . . while they threw his wife to the floor . . . whipped her . . . pinched them both with glowing pliers . . . . [The next week] several . . . groups destroyed [the castle]. All wallpaper, beds, chairs, drapes . . . tapestries were torn down . . . paintings were damaged . . . the beds, mattresses, blankets were taken. . . . the servant houses were left demolished . . . . From the . . . gardens they took the carriages . . . [the Gardener] was . . . held over a fire in his living room to give them more money. The gardener's wife was separated from her husband . . . by four Cossacks who mistreated her in a most beastly way.[29]

Letters from her relatives told Elisabeth she would hardly believe the horror stories or the ruined condition of the place. Two dismal years would go by before she saw it herself. In that time Prussian troops took one blow after another, and at one point Fritz was so beaten down he considered suicide. In the end he and his nearly bankrupt country were saved by an ironic twist of fate when of one of his petticoat enemies, the Tsarina Elisabeth of Russia, died.[30] Her successor and adopted heir was thirty-four year old Peter III, a man of dim brain, boorish nature, childishly obsessed with military parades, horseback heroes and showy victories. Of all people, he was a particular fan of the king of Prussia in spite of his aunt. When power and the crown were finally his, he turned the tables on her plans and pulled Russia out of the war as if he were manipulating his toy soldiers on his make believe field of battle. It was the only significant action of his five month reign. His wife, the new Tsarina Catherine II tolerated him until the palace guard, with her connivance, strangled him and proclaimed her the sole ruler of Russia in her own right.

---

[29] Friedrich Ludwig Müller, "Elisabeth Christine - Königin von Preußen (IV) Das ist Ihre Königin" Monumente 11/12 (1999), 62-63.
[30] Her hatred of Fritz was personal as well as political.

CHAPTER NINE

REBUILD AND REGROUP

Older, wiser and marked by physical decline, Fritz finally came home to Berlin at the end of March 1763. After seven hard-slogging years on battlefields from East Prussia to the Netherlands and Brandenburg to Bavaria, peace had been signed in Paris six weeks earlier between France, England and Spain. Prussia and Austria followed five days later in Hubertusburg in Saxony. All were exhausted and Austria faced financial default. Prussia was little better off, her treasury down by three and a half million thalers. But Silesia was secured within Prussia's borders and, more decisive, Austrian hegemony over central Europe was finished.

Fritz notified Elisabeth that her return to Berlin from Magdeburg could begin in March, but departures of her train should be spaced out; there was a considerable shortage of horses due to the war. He wanted his own homecoming played down knowing he looked more of a wreck than he had described himself in a letter to Madame Camas three years before.

> I tell you, I lead a dog's life and I suspect that only Don Quixote has ever known this kind of existence, with its endless disorders. It has aged me so much that you would scarcely recognize me. My hair is completely grey on the right side of my head. My teeth are breaking and falling out. My face is as deeply folded as the flounces on a lady's skirt, my back is bent like an archer's bow, and I go about as gloomy and downcast as a Trappist monk.[1]

All he wanted was to skulk through Berlin's back streets and not expose himself to staring eyes. Elisabeth was told to gather his brothers and their wives and children, and make sure that Camas was there as well. Most of them had not seen him face to face for seven years. He greeted his wife with a harsh comment that she was fatter. Possibly seeing her well-kept and fed was galling.

---

[1] Christopher Duffy, <u>Frederick the Great: a Military Life</u> (New York: Atheneum, 1986), 232. from <u>Oeuvres de Frédéric le Grand</u> (1846-57) Berlin XVIII. 145.

They were now fifty-one and forty-eight, well into "middle age" for those days. However, battlefield success demanded backing up by finding solutions to his depleted country's problems. Food was the immediate need; supplies were dangerously low. Army warehouses must be opened, particularly to the peasants who could not stand at the end of the food line and be expected to work on empty stomachs. Crops must be planted and help to farmers given priority. Thalers were tight in his war-stressed economy, but at the same time Prussia must fill the part of Europe's rising star, so a balancing act was required. He was sure he could accomplish that if he climbed back at once onto his treadmill of a throne.

Elisabeth's duties remained the same, holding court three times a week, and hosting official receptions and celebrations. Beyond such "window dressing" she faded onto the back burner of Fritz's life like the useful servant she had been for twenty-three years. It was hard. Luise Amalia had been living with her off and on for more than fifteen years, enduring a hard road most of that time herself, losing a husband in 1757 and a son in 1767. The sisters were greatly supportive of each other and helped Elisabeth rationalize: "One has to become a little of a philosopher in this world, because without this, one would be constantly in worries and be in a bad mood."[2] Even-handed words, but they did not always keep bitterness from boiling up to the surface, as when she wrote of longing to win the Frankfurt lottery, settle her debts and wait for death to take her.

Ernst von Lehndorff, her Chamberlain beginning in 1747 and for nearly thirty years more, saw and appreciated her good side right away, but remained at his post long enough to watch the cracks open, exposing her depression and hysteria. After 10 years he wrote:

> The Queen is basically a good woman, but to be the wife of the greatest, most worthy of appreciation and most loved of kings, to that she does not match at all . . . . It is really a pity, that this Princess, who basically possesses so many good characteristics, so often gets carried away with irritability, which for a normal life would be called brutality,

[2] Paul Noack, <u>Elisabeth Christine und Friedrich Der Grosse Ein Frauenleben in Preussen</u> (Stuttgart: Klett-Cotta, 2001) 145.

and which make her estranged from so many people, who ordinarily would be devoted to her with all their hearts.[3]

His comments are weighted with the usual late medieval expectation of women. Beauty praised and prized, but exhibiting of personal feelings and slights which would not be tolerated for a minute by their male counterparts were expected to be swallowed whole in their case.

Not long before Lehndorff's writing she ran afoul of Fritz's chamberlain, Count Wartensleben, who had denied her request for Fritz's musicians to play at a Schönhausen concert. Cultural talents were regularly traded around among the royal family in every court, but Elisabeth stood just enough outside their immediate circle to make her fair game for place seekers. Noted in an earlier chapter, courtiers were shrewd about the subplots in their masters' lives and open to advancing their careers by stepping on unprotected toes. Fritz never bothered to hide his indifference to his wife, so skirting the edge of politeness to her might well be tolerated, if not winked at. Wartensleben, full of himself and his military career, took a chance on a put down, and Elisabeth had to write to Fritz about his chamberlain's presumption. He responded, belatedly,

> I did not know one word of what you have written to me. I have let him feel my indignation and hope, that he will keep himself from now on and stay inside the limits, if not . . . then it will be the best to replace him by someone else.[4]

After that, Elisabeth seated Wartensleben at a table in the back at a dinner at Schönhausen. The broad hint did no lasting good and neither of them forgot it. Lehndorff's diary notes: "The Queen hits Wartensleben with her fan, then breaks it into a hundred pieces, throws it into his face and leaves angrily."[5] After the war was over Fritz had enough truly serious problems without this and directed one of his ministers to write:

> I heard that [you] acted so impertinently toward the Queen, that she was forced to complain about [you]. I was very displeased and I advise [you] to ask for forgiveness and to consider to be more respectful.[6]

---

[3] Noack, 89.
[4] Noack, 167.
[5] Noack, 188.
[6] Noack, 188.

This was a final warning; if there was further complaint, Wartensleben would be gone. Arrogantly unable or stubbornly unwilling to mend his ways (probably both), at last he was sent packing but with enhanced rank, a remedy as old as time - kicking the problem upstairs. Fritz knew his queen's status could not be divorced from his own power and place without diminishing them both. Better to fire the servant, with a minor sop to silence any recrimination, and save royal nerves. For Elisabeth, Wartensleben's dismissal inevitably marked a setback for taking a "philosopher's" view.

As time went on and public occasions increased in Berlin, Elisabeth's rooms in the palace overlooking the River Spree were expanded, with a large Elisabeth Hall added for the courts over which she presided. She always appeared every inch a queen, tall enough to carry off the precious robes and crown jewels she wore. Fritz, although famous and respected, had no patience with what he thought was meaningless ritual and refused to be involved. Presentations, entertaining local and visiting notables, banquets, balls and concerts all were boring and not worth the time.

His credo of living for self alone was hardening and he sounded more and more like a misanthrope. "We are a poor species while we vegetate on this little atom of mud which we call the world. I am forced to revolve like a millwheel, for one is carried forward by one's destiny."[7] He trusted fewer people, and human beings in total became objects of contempt. The men of Rheinsberg days who might have coaxed him back to youthful warmth and balance were dead: Keyserlingk in August 1745, Jordan three months earlier, Knobelsdorff in 1753 and Algarotti in 1764. Voltaire followed in 1778. For the rest of his days all that mattered was the furtherance and prestige of his country and royal House.

Prussia's new look began in Potsdam as the war ended. Trumpeting the glory of Hohenzollern, the Neues Palais's two hundred rooms, ballroom and theater contained nearly every eighteenth century architectural figure and fillip, all political statement writ large. Fritz himself had only a small apartment there, for convenience, when he was forced to preside at certain diplomatic rituals. The rest of the time he was at

---

[7] Robert B. Asprey, <u>Frederick the Great *The Magnificent Enigma*</u> (New York: Ticknor & Fields, 1986), 577.

Sans Souci, not far away, until winter set in when he moved into the Potsdam city palace.

Schönhausen benefitted from the crews of builders, artists and artisans working at the Neues Palais beginning in 1764. Fritz had promised that Elisabeth's summer place would be restored after the wreckage created by the Russians in 1760, with funds especially allotted to her, easier heard than received as usual. However, this time at the start she asked the Budget Ministry to enlarge the building in light of the public functions Fritz expected her to take on. As a result her house eventually doubled in size. A staff of fifty including her Chief Steward and Head Mistress, other ladies and personal servants were housed there and at times also important visitors. Luise Amalia and eventually Prince Henry's wife Wilhelmine became permanent residents as well, forming the trio of wedded war widows.

The ground floor was her personal space with rooms also for Mme. Camas. A large audience chamber anchored the northeast corner and diagonally opposite in the southwest corner Elisabeth's cedar cabinet or boudoir looked out on a small grove of trees. Adjoining it was the cedar paneled gallery hung with portraits of her family, living and dead, and her husband. Informal and personal, it became more and more a refuge and the portraits surrounding her of those living or passed on, a comfort.

However, in 1764 state money did not flow in like summer wine, and bills had to be met from a shallower pocket. Plain to see, corners were cut in every area, building materials and decorations, even in her kitchen. One member of her staff came to expect pretty poor fare at her table, and not much of it. In all, grandeur was not found at Schönhausen, but warmth and spirit were more her style anyway.

Rumblings of a new age had begun for her Wolfenbüttel family since 1767 with the death of Luise's second son, twenty year old Prince Henry from smallpox. His older brother Frederick William, heir to their uncle Fritz, was a skirt chaser like his father, August William, and his marriage in 1765 had foundered almost from the beginning. Fritz had arranged it as he had done for William, pulling a spirited and intelligent princess out of the family bag: his sister's daughter would marry Elisabeth's sister's elder son.

The bride, Elisabeth Christine Ulrike, was a woman several centuries ahead of her time. Once she found her self-indulgent bridegroom was not about to give up his roving ways she decided to taste for herself the sauce of the gander after their only child, Frederike, was born in 1767. Her adventures led to a pregnancy in 1769, which crossed the line of continuity for Fritz's brothers Henry and Ferdinand, whose places in the succession were thus put at risk. Fritz's scheme had messed up big time, underestimating Ulrike and cocksure that she would give in and play the dynastic game in spite of her resentment. Divorce was the only remedy, i.e. cut their losses and run. Frederick William, the vital heir, received a tap on the wrist so long as he remarried and fathered a legal heir.[8] Ulrike paid the real price: sent under house arrest into exile in Stettin, 80 miles (128 km.) to the northeast. She never saw Frederike again.

Elisabeth would have ached over this situation and most particularly for Luise Amalia. A son's dismal integrity coupled with a niece's fiery retaliation when the two were married to each other and parents of a child wounded spirits among all the joined families. Nonetheless, she would not give up her loyalty to Fritz in spite of his heavy punishment. She had always been the peacemaker growing up among her siblings, and continued to respond in the same vein to anything he asked of her. She really had no choice.

The cutting reference to her weight in 1763 and a letter of 1776 seem at odds, until the last sentence. He wanted something.

> Madam, I hear you are incommoded by a fever. If you become better and your health be restored would you make me the joy to come to Berlin but if you are ill, perhaps you should rather remain in Schönhausen; I would, of course certainly appreciate much, being in a quandary, when the Grand Duke Paul of Russia is received.[9]

Receptions had become her stock in trade; meeting important guests of the state was a job she learned to do quite well. In Paul's case, it was

---

[8] Later he contracted marriages "of the left hand", i.e. bigamy, with at least two of his favorites.

[9] Alfred P. Hagemann, "Der König, die Königin und der preußische Hof," Friedrich300 - Colloquien, Friedrich der Große und der Hof. 10 June 2010,29. <http://www.perspectivia.net/content/publikationen/friedrich300-colloquien/friedrich-hof/Hagemann_Zeitung > (14 September 2010).

déjà-vu since he was the son of her young visitor to Schönhausen in August of 1740, the future Catherine II of Russia. Like his star crossed father, Peter III, Paul was a great fan of Fritz, and the visit would be a dream come true for the difficult twenty-two year old. It was a necessary nuisance but a pain; however, for once Elisabeth at least got some acknowledgement for helping out. She arrived in Berlin the following day.

The 1770's began Schönhausen's royal heyday. Its country setting by Pankow and the pleasure garden were quiet, cool retreats for her family and other visitors. After some years the garden was opened to the townspeople as well. Indoors, the most charming element in her new palace was, and remains, its double stairway with curving, carved balusters leading from the ground floor to the second floor reception rooms. Not a genuine echo of the grand stairways at the Neues Palais of course, it was more like the workmanship found in middle class houses of Berlin at the time, and what her limited funds could afford. Ironically, however, in its small way it pointed forward toward the comfortable, elegant coziness of the Biedermeir style which was to become popular in the next century.

Fritz's reliance on his wife did not stop with her advancing age. When she was sixty-five in 1780 he asked for her help to resolve a problem he had set in motion: he was in need of a foster mother.

> There is still this poor child who has been left . . . and now can find asylum with you. You would do a great favor for me, if you would care for her, just as her passed-on grandmother [Luise Amalia] did up to now. You can easily imagine the reason which I have, to bring this business to an end. The apartments in the [Berlin] castle do not offer any difficulties, and one could under the pretense of attachment, which you have felt for the dead Princess, guide into the paths . . . .

a few days later he added:

> After I had surveyed the castle, I have . . . found the rooms . . . which one could give to the little one. . . . I shall have them made ready so the little one can move into it tomorrow.[10]

---

10 Noack, 204.

The little one was thirteen year old Frederike, Elisabeth's great-niece and her sister's granddaughter, who was to remain in Elisabeth's charge for the next eleven years. Luise Amalia had died in early January of 1780 making Frederike's vulnerable situation the King's responsibility, which he handily passed on to his wife with a plea to "please take Frederike under your wing."[11]

It cannot have been an onerous task; Luise and Elisabeth had been living together ever since William's death in 1757 and even before during the years Luise and her husband were estranged. Losing her was a wrenching setback and Frederike would be a great comfort. Further, it displayed Fritz's reliance on his wife to tie up the loose ends of family complications, a service she never ignored.

---

[11] Noack, 204.

CHAPTER TEN

DUST TO DUST

Elisabeth fell seriously ill shortly after the Grand Duke Paul's visit to Berlin in 1776. Fritz's call for help had been answered promptly as always but when the visit ended she was very tired, and Fritz was alarmed, writing to his own doctor:

> I recommend to you, to visit the Queen without delay . . . with both the other physicians in Berlin, to give her all those healing remedies . . . which you have, . . . and which demand your artistic skill. . . . we are dealing here with the most precious and most necessary person for the State, for the poor and for me.[1]

Another doctor appeared at Schönhausen within days and gave Fritz a dispiriting report. Elisabeth knew she was in a bad way when Fritz's letter had arrived, but still wanted to respond to any request, no matter how impersonal. It was the only connection she had left with him. The last words in his letter to the doctor gave away his panic, for her and probably for himself and his own wellbeing.

Ultimately she recovered, but in the process of getting back on her feet she had to face what her life had become. Restless nervousness, relentless stress over money, and implacable exile from the one human contact she desired, all had accumulated to bring her down. For the past twenty years, Fritz had walled himself off from everyone and everything that did not invigorate or intellectually feed him, his wife most of all. She was no more than his stand-in, very cold comfort to her no matter how vital she knew she was. Freed from matters not requiring his presence, his days were filled with promoting his plans to maintain what Prussia had become. The non-essentials could be foisted off upon his wife.

Elisabeth was not without moral resource, in spite of the judgment passed on her by her husband. She possessed the bedrock of her Lutheran roots and upbringing. That reality had rescued her very many times when bitter memories came back to haunt. Still, she loved him

---

[1] Paul Noack, <u>Elisabeth Christine und Friedrich der Grosse: ein Frauenleben in Preussen</u> (Stuttgart: Klett-Cotta, 2001), 177.

and accepted the way things were: wife yet non-wife queen yet absent king. More than forty years of marriage had been chilled by tacit orders to "stand here, go there, keep quiet." What had kept her spirit from total decay was poring over the works of preachers and theologians she came to know in Berlin. Her own life of the mind, independent of ceremonial obligations, began to grow as she changed focus, backing away from public ceremonials to use her energies for more real benefit, to herself and increasingly to her family and other seekers.

Always a reader, in Rheinsberg she had picked up Fritz's zeal for the works of ancient authors - Cicero, Tacitus and Marcus Aurelius as well as contemporaries Christian Wolff and Alexander Pope. Back then, Fritz had been pleased with her efforts and willing to talk them over with her. After 1740 when their daily lives totally parted she continued alone. Every week included Sunday worship at the Berlin Cathedral, across the street from the palace, where she lived most of the year. Becoming close to pastors there as well as other clergy in the capital, she invited them into her home in Berlin or at Schönhausen for dinners and table talk. They knew that her encouraging interest in their work was real, and over the next years she hosted Consistory meetings of ministers and lay people in Berlin and financially supported several congregations there from her limited income.

In summers the Cedar Cabinet at Schönhausen became study and workroom where she spent hours at her desk, writing and translating from French into German. Fancy dress balls for a body that now found walking difficult were traded in for her new passion. Instead of elegant entertainments she kept human contacts open by inviting her neighborhood into the park at Schönhausen, remarking how much pleasure she had seeing them from her windows. Giving to churches in Berlin and Schönhausen from her small purse would not win points from her atheist husband, but neither that nor enforced economy reduced her gifts. The Queen she had been, royally robed and elegantly dressed, gradually gave over to the Authoress and Translator, roles she put mind and heart into and they flourished in just the kind of life she had.[2]

---

[2] See Paula Joepchen, <u>Die Gemahlin Friedrichs des Grossen Elisabeth Christine Als Schriftstellerin</u>, (Köln: M. Mundelsee, 1939) for a complete bibliography of Elisabeth Christine's publications.

August Friedrich Sack was a preacher and member of her party that first had fled the capital to Magdeburg during the Seven Years War. Away from Berlin's formality and living in a tenuous situation, their friendship developed based on her studies and questions and his stance between the poles of rigid orthodoxy and the new rationalism. Like herself he had a traditional lodestar within that kept his faith steady, but not insular. Also while in Magdeburg she invited Anna Louisa Karsch, a Silesian poet, into her home. This was guaranteed to please Fritz, who had recommended Karsch's poem "A Widow's Complaint" to her as well as other hymns of praise to himself. Along with literary skill Karsch could improvise a poem on almost any word, similar to the musical ingenuity of Johann Sebastian Bach which Fritz had tweaked years before in Rheinsberg.[3] Sack, by contrast with the poet, a man of genuine eminence, returned to Berlin with the court and in time became the cathedral preacher.

After the war Madame Camas had recommended a French work on solitude and the inner life to her.[4] Inspired to translate it from the original German of Martin Curgot, she was able to give it to Fritz in French, the only language he saw fit to read. Though it is difficult to picture him poring over something with a Christian base, Camas' name and Elisabeth's efforts combined to engage him. Sophie Caroline Camas passed away in July of 1766 to Elisabeth's great sorrow and loss. For twenty-four years Camas had helped her navigate a sane course through difficult times in the family and in the war. No one knew Fritz much better, valued his brilliance and determination but also sympathized with the havoc those qualities had wrecked on Elisabeth.

However bereft she was, the loss probably pushed along an emerging determination of her own. Working on Curgot's "<u>Der Christ</u> . . . ," put her sadness in perspective and she could sublimate her grief. At the beginning she intended only to share it with friends, but in 1776 it appeared in print with a lengthy dedication and tribute to her brother Ferdinand. Near the same time came <u>Weise Entschließung</u>, (Wise Resolu-

---

[3] See James R. Gaines, <u>Evening in the Palace of Reason Bach meets Frederick the Great in the Age of Enlightenment</u> (New York: Harper Perennial, 2005), 8-10. Bach's genius was well beyond Fritz's ability to tarnish, down to the present day.

[4] Martin Curgot, <u>Der Christ in der Einsamkeit</u>, (Breslau: 1758), Curgot's original. (The Christian in Loneliness).

tion), her own words put down following the death of Sophia Dorothea nineteen years before.[5] At last she was finding her stride on her own.

In the 1770's Anton Büsching, an important theologian and geographer came into her circle in Berlin as well as Schönhausen. A professor of theology in Göttingen, he had been called to St. Petersburg in 1761 to pastor the Lutheran church there and in time, returned to Berlin, heading the Consistory as well as a Gymnasium (high school). In the 1750's he had published his Erdbeschreibung, commended by scholars as the first geography of Europe with sound scientific merit.[6] The book was a landmark and his presence at her table certainly elevated the boredom complained of by Lehndorff. Sans Souci was no longer the only province of intellectual conversation, particularly after the Rheinsberg friends and fellowship surrounding Fritz dwindled.

Six sermons of Johann Spalding, pastor of St. Nicholas Church in Berlin, were translated into French under her own name in 1776. Fritz thought highly of Spalding, an intellectual who espoused enlightened principles, especially when he backed up his beliefs with actions. Elisabeth favored him as well, listening to his sermons at St. Nicholas Church and translating his On the Destination of Man,[7] into French which she published under her own name in 1776 and again in 1796 the year before her death.

During the same period Fritz, who never left off his suspicious nature, was eyeing his neighbors Russia and Austria, looking for signs of oneupmanship. Maria Theresia was in a bind after her husband, the Emperor Francis I, died at age 57 in 1765. He had held the male-only imperial title since 1740, while his wife held actual power. It was a partnership that worked very well once she learned he was a failure at leading her army but very talented at managing her money. The bind, then, was not widowhood per se but having to share her power with the eldest of their sixteen children, twenty-four year old Joseph, in the newly created role of Co-Regent. Joseph, a "Starrkopf" (stubborn mule) according to

---

[5] Published as Sage Résolution de feu la Reine, (Berlin: Decker, 1776).

[6] Anton Busching, Erdbeschreibung, (Hamburg: 1769-1773). The first scientific "earth description" had demonstrated the anomalous nature of the term Holy Roman Empire of the German Nation. It was a political, not a national unit, until 1871.

[7] Johann Joachim Spalding translated by Elisabeth Christine as De la destination de l'homme, (Berlin: Decker, 1776).

his mother, was a well-educated, true believer convert to the reform ideas of the Enlightenment. Melding her traditionalist values with his liberal impatience quickly became a tractor-pull between them.

Joseph was awed by Frederick's reputation, in spite of his mother's antagonism, and eager to meet him in 1769 to deal with the implications of Russia's takeover of the Polish state, a so-called "Protectorate." Fritz and Joseph, and Maria Theresia back in Vienna, needed a candid discussion of their options to balance Russia's determined surge outward from its own borders, already heading south toward the Ottoman Empire. Eventually the three powers, Austria, Prussia and Russia agreed between themselves on a land-grab partition of Poland in 1772, a signal to Catherine II's Russia that their western expansion would not go unchallenged.

As Joseph became surer of himself, he grasped opportunities to gain territory east and west, the latter into Bavaria late in 1777. When that happened, Fritz realized Habsburg ambition was alive and well and now putting Prussia's interests in jeopardy. There was nothing for it but to mobilize his troops and challenge Joseph in what became a sixteen month war of raids and skirmishes ending in 1779 with Austria backing down and out of what she had occupied. It had been into the saddle again for sixty-five year old Fritz, to protect what he and his Prussians had grabbed.

Elisabeth pitched in early on to give her own support with <u>Réflexions Sur Affaires publiques en 1778</u> (Reflections on the State of Public Affairs in 1778) published by the king's printer that year.[8] In it she calls up her readers' courage, reminding them that God had given them a king who never spared himself risk or exhaustion; they must show confidence in victory. A short eight pages, it was more of a brochure aimed at those who were fearful about what could happen within Prussia's borders. They need not have worried. Fritz's earthy summation in a letter: " . . . may the Holy stomach of His Imperial Majesty (Joseph) return this Bavaria which he has swallowed too quickly; and which is giving him indigestion,"[9] is exactly what happened. It was Fritz's last war and

---

[8] Elisabeth Christine Queen of Prussia, <u>Réflexions sur l'etat des affaires publiques en 1778</u>, (Berlin: Decker, 1778).

[9] quoted in Giles Macdonogh, <u>Frederick the Great</u>, (London: Phoenix Press, 1999), 373-374.

once home from it he began to write a history of his reign from 1774-1778, adding the recent events of 1779.

Busy herself, Elisabeth was translating Richard Jones' Friendship with God into French and saw it published in 1778.[10] Luise Amalia's other granddaughter Wilhelmine was confirmed that year and the scholarly work was dedicated to her. The girl was headed for yet another dynastic marriage, and Elisabeth offered it as a way to ease the frustrations ahead for Wilhelmine.

Fritz plainly showed the rigors of an aging body now, seen in a portrait of 1782,[11] his mind still sharp and intact, but a surly, uncaring glint in his eyes. He did manage to visit Elisabeth and his family in her rooms at the Berlin palace on January 18th in 1785 on the occasion of his brother Henry's birthday.[12] Some of the guests may have missed him as he was in and out before most knew he was there. Henry had been a thorn in his side ever since William's death, blaming Fritz for piling on crushing words, and the rift was past mending. It was the last time Elisabeth and most of them saw him, and for Henry a bitter sweet memory.

Renowned as a legend, his health was failing. In September he suffered an apparent stroke, attacks of gout, even a bout of whooping cough. In spite of it all he kept to his daily routine, rising early and at his desk until mealtimes. Diet was a capricious regimen; over time the discrimination of his palate probably withered, since requests for hotter and spicier fare was reported by a dinner guest, when the eel patè looked "as if it had been cooked in Hell."[13]

He had given up on his doctors, preferring his own ideas and remedies, and sending both men back to Berlin. Hearing of George III's noted physician, Johann Georg Zimmermann living in Hannover, Fritz wrote to him requesting a visit, if the king of England would allow it. Permission was granted and Zimmermann appeared at Sans Souci on June 22nd in 1786. Besides oppressive asthma and gout mentioned in Fritz's letter, Zimmermann observed his patient's swollen legs and belly as well as his yellowed skin. Fritz was sitting in a chair when Zimmermann entered

---

[10] Elisabeth Christine, L'homme ami de Dieu, (Berlin: Jacques Decker, 1778.
[11] Noack, 197
[12] Noack, 196.
[13] MacDonogh, 379.

his room, saying he did not use his bed any longer because breathing was a problem. As it was, he coughed constantly and brought up small amounts of blood during their first conversation. He told the doctor he could not be cured, to which Zimmermann, according to his own report, said the king could at least be relieved.[14]

However, the problem was largely Fritz himself; Zimmermann's dosings would not be obeyed after the first trial and then were blamed for increased pain and exhaustion, only relieved by the king's lackeys holding him up while his head sagged onto his chest. After administering a clyster or enema to open the stomach, Zimmerman finally left Potsdam on 10 July. Elisabeth received no word in all this final struggle until the day before his death.

There had been no formal recognition three years earlier of their golden wedding anniversary beyond a gold commemorative coin being struck; there was no word now. Realizing she would probably be refused admittance at Sans Souci, she sent a letter instead and received a pitiful reply, "Madame, I am most obliged to you for the good wishes you deign to send, but the massive fever which I have prevents me from giving you an answer." He had already written to his remaining sisters, Charlotte and Amalia, that "the old must make room for the young."[15]

Burial under the front lawn at Sans Souci, alongside the graves of his four much beloved whippet dogs was all he wanted at the end, which came at 2:20 am on August 17th. His own directions belied reality: "I lived as a philosopher, and want to be buried as such . . . I do not want to be dissected nor embalmed, . . . want a coffin, which I have constructed, buried on the terraces of Sans Souci."[16] The markers are in place there today along with the graves of his four whippet dogs as he wished, but his heir, Frederick William II, thought all that unfit and disrespectful and later ordered Fritz's coffin taken to the Garrison Church in Potsdam to lie alongside his father. Tradition was preserved; three weeks after his death his funeral was celebrated there. Retreat

---

[14] Johann Georg Zimmermann, <u>Doctor Zimmermann's Conversations with the Late King of Prussia, When he attended him in his last illness a little before his death. To which are added several curious particulars and anecdotes of that extraordinary prince</u>. Trans. from the last edition. (London: C. Foster, 1791.), 15.

[15] MacDonogh, 384.

[16] Noack, 209.

from history, however, could not be achieved so deftly with a genius of Fritz's caliber.[17]

The will had been signed years before in 1769 with the request to his heir that Elisabeth be allowed an apartment in the Berlin palace as well as her summer home at Schönhausen. At the time she had been given a yearly 10,000 thalers and supply of wood and wine with the understanding that she would make Frederick William II, her heir also. Reaching into the future he also directed his nephew to "give the Queen, my wife, the respect which is owed as widow of his uncle and as a princess whose virtue has never been contradicted."[18] Reportedly, it was the only time he referred to Elisabeth as "wife."

Elisabeth did not visit Sans Souci after Fritz died, although she wrote to her brother Ferdinand "there is not one day that I do not shed tears for the dear, incomparable King. And as long as I live, I will not stop to shed them."[19] Elegant Sans Souci was never intended for her to share, now it was too late for any meaning. She did have a part in his final journey, though, by returning the jewels from the crown of Prussia that had been removed for her use when they married, to their original place. Thus restored, it followed his coffin in the funeral procession.

Her loss signaled the end of the past, if not its tears. The new reign let in a brighter future of warm friendship and acceptance by the new king of Prussia, the son of her departed sister Luise and father of her "foster child" Frederike. Long the good old queen to the country, her popularity during the war years was still warm. Frederick William II had always been considerate and kind and now he was the first of the family to pay his respects to her at Schönhausen three days after Fritz's death. Four days later the rest of the family arrived, all, including the servants, dressed in black.

It was a preview of the formal mourning reception held six weeks later at the Berlin Palace in Elisabeth's apartment. She stood near the throne under a canopy with only a few candles for light and the whole

---

[17] MacDonogh, 9. During the Second World War Fritz's body was removed for safekeeping to the ancestral Hohenzollern castle of Hechingen near Stuttgart. After the war and following the reunification of Germany, Fritz finally went into the grave he had chosen next to his dogs at Sans Souci.

[18] Noack, 212.

[19] Noack, 208.

company dressed in black. The solemn memorials were finally complete the next day when Elisabeth and her court paid a return visit to the new queen, Frederike of Hesse-Darmstadt, wife of Frederick William II since 1769. Drawn out ceremonies after a death in the eighteenth and even the nineteenth centuries appear barely sincere today, with their emphasis on form and fashion. Modern reality, however, appeared as the new queen moved into Elisabeth's palace suite in Berlin and Elisabeth had to move upstairs into the Swiss salon on the third floor.

A new tone invaded court society with Frederick William. Unlike Fritz, who had spared neither himself nor the rest of the family where duty was at stake, this man had developed a lack of restraint lifestyle after the manner of his unfortunate father. Women were necessary to his nature; that had doomed his first marriage and though his second wife produced four sons and two daughters, assuring the line, he continued to look farther afield to savor the good life with his mistresses. That was not all; there were innovations and reforms in the strict policies Fritz had developed which eroded Prussian financial stability. Elisabeth saw both tendencies and was shocked by them, but "the king is dead; long live the king" had always ruled and she must accept it.

Transition to actual widowhood was not easy. Her family's support had always made up in many ways for an indifferent husband, but now that was ebbing away. Death had taken six of Elisabeth's siblings beginning with her brother Friedrich Franz who fell in the Seven Years War. Five more followed before 1786. Three of them were especially close, Karl, Anton Ulrich and beloved Luise Amalia who had been her ally and constant companion for thirty-eight years. Her own death might not be far off; to have another decade of life would have seemed quite impossible. Always prudent, she set down her own last will and testament on the last day of February, 1787, ten years before it was finally needed.

> When I have gone from this world and my soul is in blissful eternity, so it is my will that my body will not be opened, and keep my nightgown on and dress it in linen cloth, and on the head a night headgear, which I wear in the mornings. My casket shall be lined totally with scent and a totally ordinary casket out of oak or stained black and with silver-plated handles. I demand that I am not put into a pa-

rade, and not to be seen by one human being, only those who cannot help it to be with me, and not to be buried too early, if it is possible, and begin eight days after my death, it is also my wish to be buried totally in quietness, my Court Staff can follow me, one can carry me, if it is not too heavy for the bearers, because it is close to the Dom, then I can be carried, otherwise if one wants to put on a wagon, and it is my will and last request, that no public ceremony may be made. This is my last Will.

Elisabeth Christine, Berlin, the 28th of February 1787.

[written in German][20]

Fortunately, nineteen year old Frederike would be with her for another five years before marrying.[21]

Getting the rest of her books into print kept her mind occupied. Besides translating a handbook of religion in two volumes by Johann August Hermes in 1784 and re-issuing it in 1788,[22] she had tried her hand at resolving the enigma of her husband with her faith in an unswerving, all seeing divine planner. Some of this rationalization reads as pietistic emotion mixed with altruism to a modern reader, but it validates a long-tried spirit like hers was.

Translating Christian Fürchtegott Gellert's "Hymns and Sacred Odes" into French was her last published effort in 1789,[23] three years after Fritz's death, and lauded at the time for expertly drawing out Gellert's meaning. He was a well-known poet and philosopher, born the same year as Elisabeth, who espoused the same Christian view of divine planning and underscored her point in Réflections . . . years before about Fritz himself being a significant element in God's design.

As time and enthusiasm kept her chained to her desk, she spoke of her labors as a calling and her epitaph.[24] It also makes plain to historical detractors of later times that she was neither ignorant nor insipid nor a

---

[20] Noack, 210.

[21] Friederike married into the extended family of Hanover and Hohenzollern, to Frederick, the second son of George III of England.

[22] Johann August Hermes, Handbuch der Religion, (Berlin: Decker, 1784 & 1788).

[23] Christian Fürchtegott Gellert, Hymnes et Odes Sacrées de C. F. Gellert, (Berlin: Decker, 1789).

[24] Alfred P. Hagemann, <a.hagemann@spsg.de> "Königin Elisabeth Christine und ihr Schloss Schönhausen, 1740-1797"). Personal e-mail (29 September 2009).

nonentity, all charges carelessly leveled against her. Indeed she was no "dumme Ding!"[25]

Her books were treasured by those of her family still living, brothers Ludwig Ernst and Ferdinand and sisters Queen Juliane of Denmark, Sophie Amalia and Therese Natalie, Abbess of Gandersheim, the latter writing "the book will eternally be a precious memory of my sister."[26] Altogether, she published a dozen translations of sermons, hymns and meditations between 1776 and 1789. Any notice or approval from Fritz had never come. None of her books are in his collections nor in the royal library in Berlin. But the French, of whom he was so inordinately fond, from afar anyway, were not so ungenerous. The Bibliothèque Nationale in Paris has all of her works.

He did leave instructions with his heir for her maintenance in the official role she continued to fill. A significant part of the ten thousand thalers a year would clear her debts, most of which were leftovers from earlier times, in which he had an indirect part. She had already completed her part of that bargain by naming the new king her heir. Her compliance should not imply approval of Frederick William II's lifestyle. Along with his legitimate family of seven sons and daughters by two wives, she accepted the two "left hand" connections he made along the way, one of them her chamber maid Julie von Voss. In the weeks before her death she received his other morganatic wife. Peace was more important now than worldly struggle and in any case, the king was both friend and nephew and she was the nearest family he had.

With the collected portraits of all her family to surround her in the Cedar Cabinet where her reading and writing continued, it was a safe haven in 1789 as she learned of the " . . . terrible catastrophe in Paris . . . . It is incomprehensible that monsters could be found, who dare speak such a sentence to someone innocent, who was their King."[27] The old model, in place for millennia, was shattered and now she was living on the downslope of that watershed. By February of 1793, as she wrote the letter it was obvious that there would be no turning back of the clock.

---

[25] (stupid thing) Joepchen, 44.

[26] Joepchen, 42.

[27] Noack, 221. Louis XVI had been executed. Marie Antoinette would follow him nine months later.

1797 began with illness in Berlin. In less than two weeks it was over; the "good old Queen" was gone and little memory of her would survive. Her brother-in-law Henry mourned in a letter to his brother Ferdinand:

> It grieves me that the good old Queen has died. I remember the dress she wore, the day of her grand entry into Berlin, sitting in a phaeton at the side of the Queen-Mother, sixty-four years ago. That impression remains. But everything passes. Her beauty was past. Her sad days are spent, her life ended - such is the history of the world.[28]

She had, however, survived to earn the hearts of all and she died their Queen.

---

[28] A. E. Grantham. Rococo (New York: Appleton Century, 1939), 196.

EPILOGUE
THE IRONY OF IT ALL...

By 1797 an overripe rococo court had presided in Berlin and Potsdam for a decade, and had proved that the adage "shirt sleeves to shirt sleeves" could be found in succeeding royal generations as often as in subjects' families. It echoed in the case of Frederick William II, Fritz's heir, whose womanizing ways and stubborn extravagance trampled on the "first servant of the state" ethic of his uncle in favor of self-indulgent polygamy and dabbles in occult religion. Prussian efficiency eroded, and France, militarily at least, stepped ahead. No longer was that country an anemic monarchy. After Louis XVI and Marie Antoinette's heads dropped into the basket below the guillotine in 1793 and the subsequent Reign of Terror took many more lives, emerging leadership passed into the hands of a new "Frederick the Great," the common born Corsican Napoleone Buonaparte in 1804.

Elisabeth's Fritz had a great admirer in Napoleon who often reminded his troops that Prussia's renowned king had brought about a new Europe, using a sword in the hands of a military genius. The Corsican intended that France would extend the goal. Success came quickly in the beginning, climaxing with marriage to the Emperor of Austria 's daughter in 1810 and their son and heir born the following year, all the price Napoleon demanded for Austria's surrender. It was his last good year.

So much success encouraged overweening ambition, goading him on to Russia by mid-September, but early victories soon dissolved into ruin after his Grande Armée entered Moscow. Fires began the following day and by mid-October, with the Tsar refusing to surrender in spite of his capital in smoldering ruins, Napoleon was forced to retreat by Russia's early winter. His soldiers clad in summer uniforms with dwindling supplies, retreated in a helter skelter forced march of more than 1,500 miles (2,400 km.) back to Paris, the half-million Armée shrunk to 20,000 by then. Prussia, Austria, Russia and England joined together to finish him the following year; exiled, not once but twice, by 1821 he was dead.

So much for legitimate heirs and copycat usurpers. Pandora's Box, now open for more than 30 years, was beyond closing again. Fusty conventions would not survive the forces set free by a social and ultimately, an industrial revolution nearly upon them. Muzhiks and the Intelligentsiya in Russia rose up and murdered the Romanov Tsar and his family in 1918. Slavs in Bohemia, Magyars in Hungary and Serbs and Croats in the Balkans chafed under the Habsburg emperor Franz Josef (Elisabeth Christine's third cousin) who had neither the wit nor the mental range to deal with his ethnic stew of an empire. Hohenzollern leadership was little better. Their combined hubris would ultimately bring Old Europe down. Not even the next iteration of a Frederick the Great, this time a baseborn Austrian, could save either Germany or Austria.

On the last day of April 1945 with Berlin burning down above him, Adolf Hitler shot himself in an underground bunker. He had asked an aide to take his treasured portrait of Fritz to safety once he was dead, but in the end Russian troops flooding into the city grabbed both the aide and the portrait.

Elisabeth's story does not end there even though her earthly remains were lost months before when a bomb shattered the crypt of the Berlin cathedral where she lay. Schönhausen was overrun by invading Russian troops again, as it had been two hundred years before, and commandeered by the Russian army for an officer's club. When the new German Democratic Republic was founded in 1949, the Soviet Union gave the palace and grounds as an official residence for Wilhelm Pieck, its first president. In the 1950's Ho Chi Minh, president of North Vietnam, Indira Gandhi, prime minister of India and Fidel Castro, premier of Cuba were given the hospitality of Elisabeth's old home. The decade was rounded out by Russian premier Nikita Khrushchev's visit in 1959. Pieck died a year later and the office of president died with him.

Schönhausen's glory days tarnished after that. Its last state occasion, the visit of Mikhail and Raisa Gorbachev in 1989 caused a small stir of refurbishment in their guest rooms. Under budget restrictions of the DDR, luxury of appointments had been limited by money and availability, but by then conditions in the dwindling Soviet Union afforded no great contrast. Hopefully, the Gorbachev's found some measure of what it had been over its 400 year history - a country retreat offering some of the peace Elisabeth found there in her long years of solitude. As to her place in the story of her country and dynasty, a quote sometimes attributed to Bertrand Russell is irrefutable: "War does not determine who is right, only who is left."[1]

---

[1] Bertrand Russell or Anonymous.

BIBLIOGRAPHY

ASPREY, ROBERT B. Frederick the Great The Magnificent Enigma. New York: Ticknor & Fields, 1986.

DUFFY, CHRISTOPHER. The Military Life of Frederick the Great. New York: Atheneum, 1986.

EASUM, CHESTER V. Prince Henry of Prussia Brother of Frederick the Great. Madison: The Univ. of Wisconsin Press, 1942.

ELISABETH CHRISTINE CORRESPONDENCE. Wolfenbüttel, Niedersächsisches Landesarchiv, Staatsarchiv Wolfenbüttel. 1 Alt 22 Nr. 771, 1 Alt 24 Nr. 287, 1 Alt Nr. 288, 1 Alt Nr. 289. 1 Alt Nr. 290. trans.

FRASER, DAVID. Frederick the Great. New York: Fromm International, 2000.

GAXOTTE, PIERRE. Frederick the Great, trans. By R. A. Bell. New Haven: Yale University Press, 1942.

GOOCH, G. P. Frederick the Great The Ruler, the Writer, The Man. New York: Alfred A. Knopf, 1947.

GROTE, HANS-HENNING UNTER BETEILIGUNG VON ELMAR ARNHOLD, MARK HEYER, HANS CHRISTIAN MEMPEL, SIMON PAULUS UND HOLGER WITTIG. Schloss Wolfenbüttel Residenz der Herzöge zu Braunschweig und Lüneburg. Braunschweig: Appelhans, 2005.

HAGEMANN, ALFRED P. Personal interview. 11 September 2009. Niederschönhausen, Germany.

HAGEMANN, ALFRED P. "Der König, die Königin und der preußische Hof," Friedrich300 - Colloquien, Friedrich der Große und der Hof. 10 June 2010 Seite 29. http://www. perspectivia.net/content/publikationen/friedrich300-colloquien/friedrich-hof/Hagemann_Zeitung>

HAMILTON, ANDREW. Rheinsberg: Memorials of Frederick the Great and Prince Henry of Prussia in two volumes 1 & 2. London: J. Murray, 1880.

HORN, DAVID B. Frederick the Great and the Rise of Prussia. London: The English Universities Press Ltd., 1964.

HUGHES, LINDSAY. The Romanovs Ruling Russia 1613-1917. London: Hambledon Continuum, 2009.

HURST, CATHERINE E. Elizabeth Christine, Wife of Frederick the Great, from German and Other Sources. New York: Phillips & Hunt, Cinccinnati: Walden & Stowe, 1880.

INGRAO, C. W. Habsburg Strategy Geopolitics during the Eighteenth Century. Rothenburg: Kiraly & Sugar, 1982.

KEITH, JAMES FRANCIS EDWARD. A succinct account of the person, the way of living, and of the court of the King of Prussia. Translated from a curious manuscript in French, found in the cabinet of the late Field Marshal Keith. London: J. Reason, in Fleet-Street, 1759.

MACDONOGH, GILES. Frederick the Great A Life in Deed and Letters. London: Phoenix Press, 1999.

MACLAGAN, MICHAEL. Lines of Succession Heraldry of the Royal Families of Europe. London: Orbis Publishing, 1981.

MEMPEL, DR. HANS CHRISTIAN AND KLAUS F. RITSCHER. Personal interview. 22 September 2006. Wolfenbüttel, Germany.

MITCHELL, OTIS C. A Concise History of Brandenburg-Prussia to 1786. Washington, D.C., University Press of America, Inc., 1980.

NELSON, WALTER HENRY. The Soldier Kings The House of Hohenzollern. New York: G. P. Putnam's Sons, 1970.

NOACK, PAUL. Elisabeth Christine und Friedrich der Grosse Ein Frauenleben in Preussen. Stuttgart: Klett-Cotta, 2001.

ORR, CLARISSA CAMPBELL, ED. Queenship in Europe 1660-1815 The Role of the Consort. Cambridge: Cambridge University Press, 2004.

RITTER, GERHARD. Frederick the Great A Historical Profile. Translated and with an Introduction by Peter Paret. Berkeley: University of California Press, 1968.

WEIHRICH, FRANZ. Stammtafel Zur Geschicte des Hauses Habsburg. Wien: Buchhändler der Kaiserlichen Akademie der Wissenschaften, 1892.

ZIMMERMANN, JOHANN GEORG. Doctor Zimmermann's Conversations with the Late King of Prussia, When he attended him in his last illness a little before his death. To which are added several curious particulars and anecdotes of that extraordinary prince. trans. from the last edition. London: C. Foster, 1791.

INDEX

G

T

V

W

Z

ABOUT THE AUTHOR

JEANNE CUMMINS brings twenty years of experience in teaching her university students to seek the human beings behind the trappings of power and parades. After raising three children she returned to school for her MA in European history and, over numerous trips, spent two years doing extensive historical research in Europe from Scotland to Russia. She also taught in her University of Portland's summer programs, twice in London and twice in Salzburg. In 2011 she and her husband celebrated their 60th anniversary in Italy.